Two Moms in My Heart

Teens Write About the Adoption Option

By Youth Communication

Edited by Al Desetta

True Stories by Teens

Two Moms in My Heart

EXECUTIVE EDITORS
Keith Hefner and Laura Longhine

CONTRIBUTING EDITORS
Nora McCarthy, Rachel Blustain, Autumn Spanne,
Kendra Hurley, Laura Longhine, Sheila Feeney

LAYOUT & DESIGN
Efrain Reyes, Jr. and Jeff Faerber

COVER ART
Amaury Almonte / YC Art Dept.

Copyright © 2009 by Youth Communication®

All rights reserved under International and Pan-American Copyright Conventions. Unless otherwise noted, no part of this book may be reproduced, stored in a retrieval system, or transmitted in any form or by any means, electronic, mechanical, photocopying, recording, or otherwise, without express written permission of the publisher, except for brief quotations or critical reviews.

For reprint information, please contact Youth Communication.

ISBN 978-1-933939-87-2

Second, Expanded Edition

Printed in the United States of America

Youth Communication®
New York, New York
www.youthcomm.org

Table of Contents

And Then She Was Gone, *Lishoné Bowsky* 13
   After her biological mother disappears, Lishoné has a hard time adjusting to her adoptive family.

Building Trust, Brick by Brick, *Manny S.* 19
   Manny slowly develops a bond with his foster mom, who plans to adopt him.

When I Had the Chance, I Turned It Down,
Natalie Kozakiewicz 24
   Although several people are interested in adopting Natalie and her sister, she wants to remain independent.

Finding My Father, *Dominick Freeman* 30
   After years of longing for a father, Dominick is finally adopted.

My Adoption Story: She Was White, I Was Black,
LeFonché Rawls 38
   LeFonché is devastated when her mother refuses to allow her white foster mother to adopt her.

Clean Slate, *Natasha Santos* 42
   Natasha thought everything would be better once she got adopted. Life is more complicated.

Contents

How Counseling Can Help You Adjust, *Tamara Scretching* 48
   An expert explains how therapy can help families through the adoption process.

I Lost My Brother to Adoption, *Wunika Hicks* 53
   When her brother David is adopted and she is not, Wunika loses her last connection to family.

Why Do Siblings Get Separated Through Adoption?,
Wunika Hicks 58
   Wunika interviews an adoption expert to find out why siblings are separated in the foster care system.

Saying No to Adoption, *Akeema Lottman* 62
   Although she's spent years in foster care, Akeema fears losing her identity if she is adopted.

Two Moms in my Heart, *Eric Green* 65
   Eric feels loved by his adoptive family, but still thinks often of his biological mother.

Losing My Everything, *Jarel Melendez* 72
   Jarel's grandmother adopts him after years in foster care, but they still have a rocky relationship.

Adopt-a-Teen?, *Natalie Kozakiewicz* 77
   Natalie gives suggestions on how to make teen adoptions more successful.

Looking for a Mother Who Won't Leave, *Lishoné Bowsky* 80
> *Unsure of being loved, Lishoné tests her adoptive mom and then her biological mom by acting wildly.*

Adoptive Families Need Support, *Lishoné Bowsky* 86
> *Lishoné interviews an adult expert about why it's important for adoptive families to get support.*

More Than Love, *Kathy Dugan* 89
> *An adoptive parent talks about the challenges of parenting kids who've faced multiple traumas.*

Embracing My Daughter's Children, *Bevanjae Kelley* 92
> *Bevanjae adopts her daughter's children.*

A Family to Raise Her, *Jennifer Jeanne Olensky* 97
> *As a teen in foster care, Jennifer decides to give up her baby for adoption.*

FICTION SPECIAL: Lost and Found, *Anne Schraff* 103

Teens: How to Get More Out of This Book 112

How to Use This Book in Staff Training 113

Teachers and Staff: How to Use This Book In Groups 114

Credits 116

About Youth Communication 117

About the Editors 120

More Helpful Books from Youth Communication 122

Introduction

Lishoné Bowsky went into foster care at age 2 and was adopted several years later. She saw her biological mother, Betty, for the last time during a visit at her foster care agency when she was 7. Betty brought her some strawberry wafers and then she was gone. Lishoné never saw her again.

Over the years, Lishoné would dream that Betty was looking for her and found her. But she never talked about these feelings with her adoptive family. "It wouldn't have changed the loneliness that Betty had left behind," she writes.

Like many of the teen authors in this book, Lishoné was grateful to her adoptive parents, although there was still a part of her "that was angry at having to be grateful for just being their child." Eventually, Lishoné became alienated from her adoptive family and left them at 14. In the years since she's grown a lot, but she writes that she hasn't really come to terms with her feelings about being adopted.

Complicated and divided feelings like Lishoné's are present throughout the 18 true stories in *Two Moms in My Heart*. Many of the adoptions described in this book are successful, and some teens write about finding new sources of support, love, and stability in their adoptive families. But even in the best of circumstance, the writers also experience confusion and conflict.

Teens can be particularly ambivalent about the idea of fusing with a new family. They may not be willing to give up their remaining ties to their birth families, trust a new set of parents, or make the effort to fit in to yet another family.

For example, Natalie Kozakiewicz, an orphan who grew up in poverty, turns down the chance to be adopted by a well-do-to couple. Although they seemed like "perfect parents" with a big, beautiful house, Natalie is comfortable with her decision. At this point in her life, she would rather be independent than run the risk of having to change herself to fit a new family's expectations.

In contrast, the author of "Building Trust, Brick by Brick" is happy to be adopted by his foster mom after he gradually learns to feel safe with her. And Dominick Freeman, who was abandoned by his father before he was born, finds his "dream dad" when his internship supervisor ends up adopting him.

For other writers, the resolution is less clear cut. Eric Green is torn between the security of his adoptive family and his love for his biological mother. Jarel Melendez, adopted by his grandmother, grows distant from her yet still cherishes everything she's done for him. And in "Looking for a Mother Who Won't Leave," Lishoné explains why she ended up having conflicts with both her adoptive and biological moms, and feels she can't live with either one. "I don't feel ready to tell my two moms that I love them," she writes. "Maybe I still don't trust that they love me back."

Yet most of these writers gradually come to terms with their feelings, families, and identities. Natasha Santos, after living in several uncaring foster homes, finally gets adopted by a family she likes and hopes it will be a fresh start.

"I thought that once I got adopted everything would change," Natasha writes. "I believed all my past troubles and trauma would be erased and that I would start new."

Those expectations don't come true—Natasha still feels hurt and angry after the adoption, and has a hard time telling her family about her abusive past. But, over time, they begin to listen to and understand one another, and Natasha develops the more mature realization that "I will drive myself crazy looking for families like the ones on television."

The stories in *Two Moms in My Heart* reflect how complicated the adoption experience can be, especially for teenagers. They are ideal for opening up discussions with teens and families who are have experienced or are considering adoption.

In the following story, names have been changed: *Embracing My Daughter's Children.*

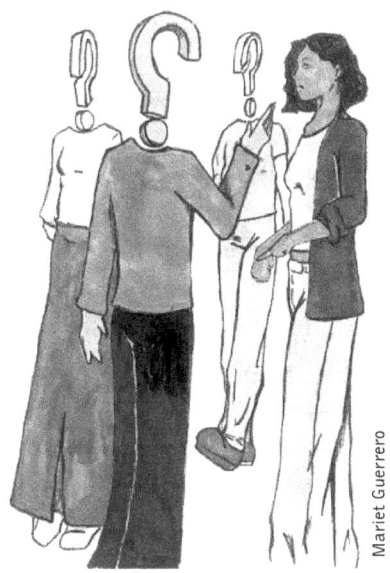

And Then She Was Gone

By Lishoné Bowsky

I am Betty Lavender's child, or at least I was. My grandmother died and my mother put drugs first, so I was put into foster care at the age of 2.

I have no real memory of Betty Lavender, just her name and the last time I saw her. I was 7 and recently adopted. But we had gone to Saint Joseph's foster care agency for a visit. Betty brought me some strawberry wafers.

I remember my adoptive mother telling me to say thank you and I did. Then Betty got up and told me she would see me again. I went back to the agency a month later for another visit, but she never showed up. My mother was gone and I was no longer her child.

I was fully aware of being adopted because my adoptive parents, who I'd lived with for the past four years, asked me how I would feel being their child, and I said I had no problem with it. So they adopted my biological sister and me at the same time.

I can remember I was happy to be adopted, but at the same time sad. I was happy because I had a family, a nice warm bed to sleep in every night, plenty of food to eat, and a place to run around. I was sad because I never got to say goodbye to Betty, and the last time I saw her I didn't take in what she looked like. I was sad because she never showed up to see me again. She had lied when she said that she would.

I'm not sure why I never saw Betty again, but for years I looked at myself as an intrusion. I figured she didn't want to see me anymore because I needed things and that would get in the way of her drug habit.

When I went to sleep, I'd have dreams that Betty had been looking for me and found me. I'd have dreams that she would recognize me and come up to me and say, "Lishoné, it's me, your mother Betty!"

But I never talked about these things. I guess I just didn't see the point. It wouldn't have changed the feeling of loneliness that Betty had left behind. Besides, I didn't even know what exactly I was feeling, so keeping my feelings inside seemed normal. But it also left me even more lonely.

My adoptive parents didn't make it that easy for me to talk, either. It wasn't that they weren't good to me. They took me on road trips down south, they took me to amusement parks, and they got my hair done every two weeks. They gave me a stable home, something I probably would have never had if I had been in foster care or still lived with Betty.

But my adoptive mother jumped to conclusions when I would try to tell her little things about boys or school or anything that happened in my life. She always assumed I was getting in some kind of trouble. So there wasn't any way I would have told her about my most painful, private thoughts, even if I had thought of telling her.

Instead, I just tried to be the nice kid who always seemed happy. I would smile, laugh and joke. I'd come home and talk about everybody under the sun and how they were doing, except myself.

I didn't want my adoptive parents to feel as if I wasn't appreciative or that I didn't love them, so I tried to act as if everything was good. When you're adopted you feel like your adoptive parents at one point or another are going to expect you to be grateful. You imagine they're thinking, "We could have left you in foster care or you could be dead right now."

And I was grateful. But there was still a part of me that was angry at having to be grateful for just being their child. There was a part of me that didn't trust their love, that said, "What makes you love me when my real mother didn't love me? What's so real about your love?"

> **When I went to sleep, I'd have dreams that Betty had been looking for me and found me.**

When I was angry I expressed my pain by either writing or acting out, or sometimes both. At school I had a quick temper. I got into physical fights and cursed people out. I ran away from home a lot, more times than I can count. My family couldn't understand why I acted the way I did, and neither could I. I just knew that I felt bad.

It wasn't until I got into my teens that I said to myself that it was Betty's loss to not know me and I wasn't going to worry about her anymore. If she couldn't take care of me then she shouldn't have had me. So what if I was an intrusion? She made me an intrusion.

If I was out in the street and the thought of Betty would enter my mind, I would turn my head and find something to distract me. If I was at home, I would get up and grab a book or watch television.

But even while I blocked out Betty, the hurt continued, and my behavior got worse and worse. I spoke whatever was on my mind and cared very little about how people were feeling. My most common response to anything anybody said to me was to curse or say "Whatever." I was rude, rebellious, and the littlest thing ticked me off. I had a non-caring attitude, and the worse I got, the more frustrated and angry my parents got.

By the time I was 12 or 13, my mother and I really weren't getting along. She often beat me and a couple of times she threw me off of the piano bench while I was practicing.

Whenever I got on my mother's nerves, she would tell me, "I don't care who you go and tell that I punished you. If they want you they can have you because I'm tired of you." Or she'd say, "I never had this problem with Sidney and Jarrod (her two biological sons). Why couldn't you be like them?"

I felt that my mother didn't want me even though she had adopted me. I felt that she wanted a replica of her children—who didn't act out so much and didn't get in trouble in school—standards I could never live up to.

The only true family I will ever have is the one that I will one day start.

It didn't help that much that my extended family never really accepted me. Every Christmas they acted funny toward me. (I found out later that some of them never wanted my adoptive parents to adopt me in the first place.)

When things got really bad with my mom, I went to one of my aunts for help and she threatened to call the police on me for running away. She didn't like me, and the truth is, she didn't like my mom either. She just didn't want to be involved.

I ran away for the last time when I was 14. Even though my mother wanted me back, I felt she had put me through too much mental, physical, and emotional anguish to return. I rejected the only family I had had for the last 10 years, a family I had come to feel didn't want me, but just put up with me.

I'm 19 now and have been on my own for the last five years. I've lived with a friend, I've lived on the streets, and I've lived in the foster care system. I've grown a lot, but I haven't really come to terms with my feelings about being given up or about being adopted.

I have friends and other people who support me now, so to a large extent, the feelings of loneliness have disappeared. But my anger has not. Instead of blocking it out, I talk to my boyfriend about it and try to make sense of it all. Maybe one day I will forgive and forget, but right now I feel like the only true family I will ever have is the one that I will one day start.

I do have some contact with my adoptive mother. Sometimes I talk to her when I call my sister, who still lives with them. My mother wrote me a letter apologizing for the past, and she has even asked if she could come to my college graduation. I'm thinking about it, but I'm not sure I can forgive her yet for all the things she said and did to me that really hurt.

I don't think I will ever forgive my extended adoptive family. They weren't there for me and my mother when we were having troubles. They didn't stick by me. They made me feel like they never wanted me.

To this day, I carry around feelings of not belonging and feelings of wanting to belong.

When I was younger I was able to block the memory of Betty out of my mind, but now it isn't so easy. I look into the mirror and I want to know who I look like. If the children I intend to have one day ask, "Mommy, what was she like, your real mother?" I want to be able to answer that. Or I'd like my kids to be able to ask her for themselves.

It feels like the chance of finding Betty are as slim as the skin peeled off an apple. I have tried to watch out for talk shows that ask the question, "Were you abandoned and want to know why?" One time I even called a talk show, but I got a machine that said, "We are currently not accepting any more calls on this topic," so I gave up on that.

I realize I may never find Betty. I'll have to accept that. Still, I want to find her, and the thought of her comes into my mind often. I am angry at her because she lied to me and I am angry because she left me. But if I found that Betty was dead or in jail, it would bring a sense of closure and fill up that empty space in my heart.

Lishoné was 19 when she wrote this story. She has since had a daughter and earned a graduate degree in public policy.

Building Trust, Brick by Brick

By Manny S.

By the time I got sent to my third foster home when I was 8 years old, I'd started to believe that all my experiences in foster care would be negative. I was trapped in a circle of revolving doors, and I didn't think I'd ever be able to stay in one place.

At my first foster home, there was a kid named Robert who thought he could bully my younger brother Daniel. One day I got so fed up with him that I punched him in the face, and my brother and I got kicked out. Then we were sent to live with my uncle, which was great, until he kicked us out. He said it was because Daniel and I were always fighting.

After getting the boot from my own family, I started to think I couldn't rely on them as much. I figured I could only be independent. I also believed that since I wasn't in those two homes for very long, my next home would be the same.

Two Moms in My Heart

On my way to my next foster home I thought I'd better be ready to leave in three or four months, and I was already worried about where I'd get sent next. I was also scared of what my new foster mom would be like. I pictured her as a witch with razor-sharp teeth and claws.

I walked to the door with Daniel and my social worker and rang the bell. I heard barking and I was terrified at what she might have in that house—perhaps a pit bull trained to scare little kids, or torture them as they slept.

The door opened and I saw a woman with a happy face, anxious but full of excitement. She welcomed us in, but I was cautious due to what I'd heard at the door. Then I looked down, and saw a little dog whose bark was way bigger than his bite.

I looked around the apartment and I liked what I saw, but I was still on my toes.

The woman said her name was Melba. She showed us our room and told us to make ourselves at home, but I didn't unpack my things just yet. I felt like there was no point since we would be leaving soon anyway. My brother and I stood in the hall as Melba and my social worker talked in the living room. I started to imagine the horrible things she would do or make us do when my social worker left.

> **I had grown to love Melba, but the idea that I couldn't live with my parents again seemed weird to me, and made me sad.**

When my social worker came in to say goodbye I thought, "Yup, this is it." I heard the door slam shut and my heart started to pound as I heard footsteps closing in toward the room, but I played it cool and sat on the bed. Her mouth opened and just when I thought she was going to breathe fire, she asked, "Are you guys hungry?"

Daniel said yes, but I said no. I was, but I wasn't comfortable asking her for anything. When she went to use the bathroom, I ran to the kitchen and grabbed a little something to eat.

The first few months were all the same. I would get home

from school, go to my room, close the door and do my homework. When Melba would come by and ask if I was hungry I'd usually say no. She didn't annoy me or force me to eat. She gave me my space, which was what I wanted. At dinnertime, I would just stay in my room.

Most of the time when I was in my bedroom, Melba would come in and ask if I'd finished doing my homework. I have to admit, it felt good to know she cared. We'd sometimes have little awkward encounters. Maybe a "Hey" or "Hi" but nothing more than that.

After five or six months, I started thinking I might be here longer than I'd thought. I also noticed Melba's consistency when it came to feeding me and checking my homework. Sometimes I'd take some change off her dresser to see how she'd react, but she never seemed frustrated.

I started to feel a little warmer inside. I began to answer, "Yes," when she asked if I was hungry, and I started leaving the door to my bedroom open. We even started to have conversations about things we liked or had in common. I found out that she'd had other foster children living there, but they were given back to their families. I thought that maybe the same thing would happen to me.

I felt happy that under Melba's care those kids had "survived" long enough to be returned to their families. I felt she could do the same for me until I was reunited with my family. This let me feel comfortable trusting Melba. Pretty soon I started to hug her when I came home from school, and I started showing her more affection than any of my previous foster moms.

On my 9th birthday, Melba took Daniel and me to the World Trade Center, which I'd never visited (this was shortly before 9/11). When we got to a huge building that towered over me, she said, "We're here." I thought that we were going to do something boring, but I was shocked when we got inside. There was actually a huge variety of shores and restaurants. I'd never seen anything like it in my entire life.

We looked everywhere and we got to eat pizza at a cool restaurant, which I wasn't used to. When we sat down I tried to think of the last time I'd eaten at a table like that. I was so happy that she remembered my birthday, took me somewhere and had gotten me a present.

After that, I opened up a lot more. I believed that Melba had paid her dues and earned her stripes as my foster mom. I started talking to Melba a lot, and I often found myself the one starting the conversations. We'd talk about the news, school, TV and anything else worth talking about. The conversations weren't three hours long, but they were progress nonetheless. I also began to get closer to her family, which was cool. They didn't live with us, but they all treated me as if I was really part of their family.

Around the time I turned 14, I realized adoption was a possibility. We didn't really talk about it, but as time went on I knew that eventually it had to happen.

One day Melba sat me on the couch and said, "If you want to be adopted, I am here for you." I had grown to love Melba, but the idea that I couldn't live with my parents again seemed weird to me, and made me sad. I had to think about my situation before I could make a decision.

For years, my birth mother had filled my head with the dream that I'd be going home. But it never happened.

For years, my birth mother had filled my head with the dream that I'd be going home. But it never happened. Every time she made a promise that I could go home and then didn't keep it, I felt knocked down to the ground. That's when my mother would come again and lift up me up, only to knock me down again. But eventually, I got used to her routine.

When I finally realized that going back home wasn't going to happen, I knew that adoption was what I wanted. Now we're in the process of making that happen.

Melba has already been my parent for so long; the only thing that the adoption will change is that my brother and I will legally belong to her. Melba has given me advice and taught me those life lessons that you need to succeed, like saving money, helping people and taking school seriously.

Melba and I have developed a bond over the past several years. I am happy that I finally got a break from the negativity, and soon it will be permanent. Melba has been my salvation from a dramatic and awful life. We started from one brick and built a skyscraper of trust, understanding and love.

Manny was 15 when he wrote this story.

When I Had the Chance, I Turned It Down

By Natalie Kozakiewicz

"Wow, can they really be taking me to lunch and giving me authentic jewelry? I just met them a few weeks ago and they're giving me gifts for my birthday, which passed six months ago. What's going on?"

The couple had given me a 14k gold chain with a real sapphire diamond on it and a pair of earrings to match. They had a nice, big house upstate where they wanted to take my sister and me, and they were planning to take us to Maine for a summer vacation.

They wanted to adopt my sister and me from foster care, and we had to decide quickly whether we wanted them to be our parents or not.

My sister and I came into foster care with no parents and no relatives anyone could find. My pops died from cancer and my moms died about two years after from a heart attack. (Both of them were alcoholics and smokers). My sister was 10 and I was 12 years old when my mother died.

When we came into care, my social worker told us that she was going to take pictures of my sister and me. I asked, "Why?" She said she needed to put our pictures in a book, "just for the record."

I didn't know that the pictures would go into a book that families wanting a child would look at. I didn't know those pictures would lead to such a serious issue—adoption.

A lot of people get foster care and adoption mixed up, but they're really very different. When you're in foster care you really belong to the city and a foster parent or group home staff are paid to take care of you.

When you are adopted, you become part of a family and no one pays that family. If the family buys you new clothes, they take the money out of their own pocket. But the main difference between adoption and foster care is that adoption is permanent and foster care isn't. If you're adopted, you're in that home for good. It's supposed to be similar to living with a biological family—you're part of the family.

About a year and a half after I took the pictures, it seemed that everyone wanted me to be adopted.

"We have a nice family for you who lives in upstate New York," my social worker asked. "Do you want to be adopted?"

"You want me to adopt you?" my adult friend, Gia asked. Gia is 33 years old and like a Godmother to me. When I lived with my mother, she lived in an apartment upstairs from us. My sister and I saw her almost every weekend when we first went into care. Now she buys me things whenever I'm in need and my foster mother doesn't help me out.

Even my best friend Monika said, "When I have more space, maybe I can adopt you, right?" And my foster mother wondered,

"Do you want to be adopted by me?"

Did I have to be adopted? Who would I choose as my family? Could I wait before deciding?

Luckily, I was old enough that they had to get my permission before anyone adopted me. My sister wasn't old enough, but they don't like to split up siblings. So I was the one who got to make the decision. But what would I choose?

Back then I thought adoption meant that I would belong to a family all over again. I thought that I could become close to that family, but not as close as I was to my real parents. Even if the new parents were great, they couldn't fully take the place of my real parents. My biological parents raised me and made me who I am today. For some family to think they could just walk in my life and claim that they're my parents made me feel uncertain about them.

Still, I thought it would be good to be part of a family again, with parents who would choose to adopt me and really care about me. But who knew if I would go into a family that really cared about me, or one that would abuse or neglect me? It was kind of like playing the lottery. I couldn't really tell what a family was like by going out to dinner with them a few times.

> *It was kind of like playing the lottery. I couldn't really tell what a family was like by going out to dinner with them a few times.*

My sister and I met with the couple from upstate New York a few times. They would ask how I was doing and they would ask about school. That made me feel like they were interested and cared about me, unlike my foster mother who never asked those types of questions. They seemed like the perfect parents since there was a mother and a father, and they were married and lived in a house. They also showed their affection by getting me gifts for my birthday, which my foster mother doesn't do.

I did and didn't want to be adopted by them. I did because it was only going to be my sister and me in a big, beautiful house.

Also, the couple seemed to really care or like us, at least more than our foster mother did.

But I didn't want to go because of how far it would be from New York City. I didn't want to leave my best friends because they have been there for me since before my mother died. One of my friends raised money for my mother's memorial and burial. And I wouldn't want to lose Gia and her boyfriend by moving somewhere far like upstate.

But most of all, the whole thing made me feel strange. I felt like the family was trying to buy us, and there was something funny about that. They would spend so much money in the little time they knew us, and we know from the Beatles that money can't buy love, and from J. Lo that love don't cost a thing.

Before I went into foster care, my mother, sister, grandmother, roommate, and I were living in the ghetto where there were drug dealers, roaches, and rats. We were in a very small, $600 apartment of three rooms. We lived off my mother's welfare check, my grandmother's social security check, and the money that our roommate sometimes gave us—basically we were poor. But if I could choose to live with someone rich or live in the ghetto with my mother, I would definitely choose my mother.

I was so confused about what to do about the couple upstate. I felt flattered that they wanted to adopt me, scared that if I turned them down I might hurt them, and worried that if I let them adopt us, they might hurt us or we might regret it.

Some people were telling me to be adopted and some were telling me not to. Gia and Andrew were telling me not to because we wouldn't be able to see them. My social worker really wanted me to be adopted. She thinks it's best for foster kids to have permanent homes and people they can turn to when they're trying to become independent adults.

I thought about it for a month. I knew it was a decision that could change my life forever. Then my sister and I decided to turn the family down. That was well over a year ago. But I still sometimes wonder about how my life would be if I were with that family.

After I turned that family down, Gia and Andrew wanted to adopt us. I know they are great people with good advice and care, but still something was holding me back. It took me a while to figure it out, but I realized that I felt I had to be the way they expected me to be or else they wouldn't like me or accept me.

It wasn't something I just felt about them. Being in foster care has taught me how to adapt to everyone's lifestyle, but I haven't yet figured out what my own lifestyle is. I felt if I got adopted, I would have to pick one person's way of living.

For example, when I go to my friend Monica's house we go to church on Sunday. If we don't, we kind of get in trouble. But in Gia's house it's the opposite—she and her boyfriend are not religious people, and they don't want my sister and me to go to church when we're with them.

When I go to Gia's, we usually watch TV, talk, and eat together. But in my foster home, I come home and go straight upstairs to my room. My foster mother and I don't eat or watch TV together. When I am with my friends I like to wear name-brand clothes, but Gia doesn't care for clothes with logos. Also, neither Gia nor Monika like the music I listen to.

So adoption was like choosing how I should be: Should I act religious or not? Should I watch TV or read a book? Should I wear this or not?

I try to be this perfect friend to everyone so that they will like me. I no longer have one clear family, so I'm always trying to adapt to my friends' lifestyles. If I got adopted, I would have one clear family. But would it be the kind I wanted?

After I turned down Gia and Andrew, I also turned down the whole idea of adoption, period. I told my social worker to change my goal from adoption to independent living. Independent living means I will live in a foster home until I'm 18 or 21, and then I'll be on my own.

Today I'm still in a foster home. I'm glad that I decided to stay in foster care because I see all my friends regularly, and if I feel my foster mother is treating me wrong, I'll be able to move. It won't be permanent. I'm also glad because when I graduate from high school, my agency will pay for my room and board in college until I'm 21.

If I got adopted, I would have one clear family. But would it be the kind I wanted?

I sometimes think about how all those people wanted to adopt me. I do think it would be great to be part of a family again—especially if the family was perfect. (Ha ha, yeah right!)

But I also don't believe that I can fully be part of a family again. Maybe it can come very close, but deep down inside I think that it can't be the same. No one can really replace the love that was between my mother and me. My mother had been there since I was born. She knew me better than myself at times, and I knew she definitely loved me. Therefore I didn't have to be a certain way for her to like me. Since I was her daughter, I knew she loved me already.

Natalie was 16 when she wrote this story. She later went to college and graduate school, majoring in anthropology.

Finding My Father

By Dominick Freeman

I had a fantasy of what I wanted in my dream dad. He would know how to make money and help me figure out how to have a successful career as an architect. He would understand that my past, which includes being beaten, humiliated, neglected, and rejected, was not my fault. My dream dad would listen and have patience with me. He would love me and respect me and I would love and respect him back. He would be there for me, forever.

I wanted a man in my life, a father figure, because I never had one. My real father left my mother before I was born. According to relatives on my mother's side, he was a gang member who gave me 22 other half-brothers and sisters.

I desperately wanted to be adopted. But I had been free for adoption since I was 8 and my first two adoptions had failed.

At age 9 I was supposed to be adopted by a nice guy called

Dave, but his other adopted son didn't want me to move in. When I was 10, my aunt Sandra and my uncle Willie, who surrendered me to foster care at age 6 due to family tension, said they would adopt me, but because they lived in Pennsylvania and I was in foster care in New York, things got complicated and they didn't. My hopes were raised and then smashed. I bounced from one foster home to another. I never stopped hurting.

When I was 15, I got a clerical job at a hospital for the summer and went to work for Richard Freeman, the associate director of psychiatry. He was a quiet, calm white guy with fewer wrinkles than your average 40-year-old. All the people he worked with talked about how great he was. Richard turned out to be a great boss, because he never yelled at me when I made a mistake.

We left work at the same time, and sometimes, after work, we'd hang out and he'd buy me ice cream or pizza. This made me even happier to have him as my boss.

At the time I met Richard, I was living with a Pentecostal woman in her mid-60s who devoted all her time to church. She cooked curried goat and white rice with coconut extract and thyme, which I thought was disgusting. A few months after I moved in, I asked her if she allowed kids to swear.

"If you swear at me," she replied. "I'll send you to another foster home and you'll never come back."

She told me another kid cursed her, so she called a social worker on him. Two hours later he left and she never saw him again. For this reason and others, I didn't trust her to become my adoptive mother. I never trusted any of my foster parents. I knew they didn't love me and might disappear any day.

My six different foster care placements included a psych ward, a horrible, strict group home, and a home with Mormons who listened to long, boring sermons for six hours every Sunday. The other six days of the week they beat me for stupid reasons with rulers, belts, and brooms.

I was glad I left their house after three years because I didn't want to be beaten to death. I was sick of living with old women and religious people. They couldn't understand why I disliked church, enjoyed rave music and metal, and wore black raver pants.

One day I asked Richard, "Do you go to church?"

"Not in many years," he said. I was shocked because everyone I had ever lived with went to church. "Well, what is your view on religion?" I asked.

"To me, church is a place where people are being controlled by fear. I don't feel that it's right for people to impose their religious beliefs on others," he explained.

That was the weirdest conversation I had ever had. A grown person shared my opinions! This made me want to draw closer to him.

Over the summer, Richard and I took the same train home each night and we got to know each other better. Every day on the train we talked about different political topics: President Bush, the tragedy of September 11th, and our corrupt government. We both agreed that we were liberals. That drew us even closer.

As our conversations became more personal, I let out my past to him and told him how I had been abused. I told Richard that I was in foster care, that I was not adopted yet, and that I would love to live with a dad, or a mom and dad. I had no idea he was actually listening to me when I talked.

One day I went into Richard's office and found him looking at an adoption website on his computer.

"Why are you looking for kids who want to be adopted?" I asked.

Richard said he was researching the topic of adoption and seeing if he was eligible to be an adoptive parent. This made me really jealous. I wanted to yell, "HELLO? Didn't I tell you that I am free for adoption? Why are you looking at all these other kids when you have me?"

Instead, I just told him, "The kids on there are no bargain, you know."

In the last week of working at the hospital, Richard and I got ice cream and sat down in a park. Richard told me about his mother. "Just like you, I had problems with my family. My mother was a person I couldn't stand to be with. I left New York six years ago to go to San Francisco and get as far from her as I could."

That explained why he understood me so well—he had problems with his family, just like I had with mine. Finally I just asked him, "Why don't you adopt me?"

> **I told Richard that I was in foster care, that I was not adopted yet, and that I would love to live with a dad.**

"Dominick, I want to tell you something," he said in a real serious manner. "I'm gay."

I had chills for a second. I had no idea! He was good looking and could have any girl he wanted. We had talked about our family relationships but not our romantic relationships, so it never occurred to me he might be gay. I had to think for a minute.

"I don't care that you're gay," I finally told Richard. "I just want you to be a good parent to me. That's what I care about the most."

"I'm not going to make any promises," said Richard. "I don't know how long adoption takes or all that's involved, but I will try. I hope one day I will have you as my son."

The week after I finished my summer job, my social worker, William, asked me if I wanted to bring Richard to a baseball game.

When I went to meet Richard at William's office, William walked up close to me, like he wanted to tell me a secret. "I don't know if you know what Richard is doing, but I'll tell you," William whispered. He sounded really, really happy. "He's in the process of adopting you! It's a good thing that you stood up and found a dad all on your own. I'm very proud of you, kid."

I told Richard this and he said, "Well, I was going to keep it a secret, but now you've found out." We laughed through the whole game.

The adoption process started in September with a home visit. I loved Richard's apartment. No roaches and no mice! My other homes had a lot of insects, especially water bugs. Richard had already set up my bedroom. I felt so welcomed when his two cats, Sheva and Thelma, wanted all kinds of attention from me. I'd never been to a nice restaurant like the one he took me to. It was a hell of a good time. What I liked most was that, for the very first time, I got to see how life can be good in New York. Everything was great. This was the right house for me. I wanted to stay as long as I could.

Finally, three days after my 16th birthday, my dad became certified as a foster parent and I moved into his house. Almost immediately, we got into a fight over my curfew, which was 5 p.m. None of my friends had to be home that early. We fought about the curfew for weeks.

Then one day I asked Rich, "If I do what I have to do this month, can I have a later curfew?" He agreed. His acting reasonable made me feel reasonable. For a whole month I came home on time. Richard extended my curfew to 9 p.m. on the weekdays and midnight on the weekends. I was satisfied.

National Adoption Day was a few months later, and that was the day Richard and I went to the courthouse to make my adoption legal. I traded my last name of Gonzalez to become "Freeman." Since that moment, I have become a new man. I feel loved and happy to be out of the system. I'm truly a free man!

Since my adoption, Richard has proven to be my dream dad, but everything has not gone the way I dreamed. Even before the adoption there was tension. I had trouble believing anyone would really be there for me in the long run, so I let out a lot of my frustrations on Richard. When Richard told me not to pour ketchup over all my food without asking or not to interrupt people, I flipped out.

When I decided I didn't want to be on anti-depressants anymore, my dad agreed to let me go off them, but I became much more irritable and slammed doors. I was scared that this adoption could fail like the first two. I also knew it would end all my hopes of being reunited with the family I was born into. My birth family would never approve of a white, gay man adopting me. I tried not to worry so much by reminding myself, "Rich has done more for me and offered me more than everyone in my family put together."

Richard wants me to be more responsible, and he still lectures me about how important it is to care about the people around you. It has taken me a long time to learn how to be selfless. But I am willing to try because I don't want to be self-centered all my life. Families can't work if each person is only thinking about himself.

I had trouble believing anyone would really be there for me in the long run.

I had to be self-centered in the past because it was part of my survival—no one else cared about me but me. But now I realize there is no longer any need to behave the way I used to. I don't have to be anxious about being heard all the time, but can concentrate on listening to others. I'm changing.

In the last few months our family has grown. Devon, my dad's boyfriend, and my new brothers, Tyrik, 15, and Derrick, 11, have moved into our four-bedroom house. Derrick, who has a lot of heart and a great sense of humor, is also being adopted by my dad. Tyrik, a foster child who just came into our lives, is also very helpful and supportive. Devon helps us boys with things like cooking and homework, and helps keep track of where we all are. I never take my family for granted.

We may not look like a traditional family—we're all guys and all different races— but in lots of ways we are.

I have chores like setting the table, taking out the garbage, and cleaning the bathroom. We go on family vacations to San Francisco, Toronto, Philadelphia, and Boston. Dad takes us away so we can all enjoy different places, but also to advance my education. He has really encouraged my goal to become an architect and is always pointing out differences in city skylines and how buildings are put together. Another difference is I don't have to eat disgusting food. We have food like chicken cutlets, ham, and yellow rice—my favorite!

Also, we celebrate traditional holidays. Christmas is one of the coolest days. Our TV shows a tape of a fireplace, and we have a Christmas tree and hang ornaments.

I can also talk to my dad about anything, including sex. I love to see how much my dad will put up with at the dinner table when I ask him raunchy questions about fantasies or fetishes, but I can also ask him about serious things like love. One time I was in a bad relationship with a girl and depressed because I felt she was controlling my life. At first my dad laughed, but I told him that was very hurtful.

He stopped laughing and said he had been in a similar relationship once and that no one deserves to be manipulated and yelled at. He told me to wait to speak to her until I was calm and to tell her how I felt. His advice helped me handle a situation that could have escalated. My dad is open-minded and sensitive to other people's problems.

My high school average is B+ and I have already been accepted into college. I want to be as successful as Richard. Because he's been my dream dad, in return I want to give him a dream son. Knowing that he will always be there for me, every day, makes me want to make him proud every day, for the rest of his life. I want to be successful, social, and cooperative. For a long time I was a hermit, but now I'm feeling a lot more communicative.

The love he has shown me has also changed my opinions of gay people.

When I was little, being called a "gaylord" or a "faggot" was a real bad thing. In care I heard all kinds of negative things about gay people. I was in a group home from age 12 to 14, and because I was physically and emotionally weak the boys there questioned my sexuality and made me feel ashamed that I knew gay people. But living with my dad has made me much more open-minded and tolerant.

Being gay doesn't make you a good or bad parent. I think what makes you a bad parent is a lack of compassion, and my dad has lots of compassion. For those who think that gay people shouldn't adopt, I have to tell you this: I've been way better off having a gay parent in my life than having two straight, abusive parents. I needed a good parent, and I finally got one.

Dominick was 18 when he wrote this story.

My Adoption Story: She Was White, I Was Black

By LeFonché Rawls

I was 11 years old when I reached my third foster home. I liked it a lot. It was on a clean and quiet block. The only problem was that my foster mother Alicia was Italian (yes, she was white) and I was black.

I first met Alicia at my foster care agency. I was hungry and tired, because I'd been waiting for hours and hours. Then she finally showed up—a tall, thin, white woman with blackish-gray hair.

I had all this hate and hostility towards white people because of my mother. She didn't like white people. She was a Muslim. She taught me that all white people were evil. So my first impressions of Alicia were "White Devil," "Rapist," and "Black Slavemaster for over 430 years."

After talking for a little while, I turned to my former foster family (who had been abusing me both mentally and physically) and said goodbye. (But in my mind, I was really saying "good riddance.") Alicia said I was beautiful, her "pretty little brown baby." Then we went downstairs to her car and drove off.

We pulled up to a two-family house. I thought it was beautiful. I thought to myself, "I always wanted to live in a house." I took a look inside and saw a beautiful upstairs and downstairs. I also saw a little brown mixed poodle and Lhasa-Apso.

The only problem was that my foster mother was white and I was black.

The excitement wasn't over yet. Charging downstairs was a big, black-and-mahogany colored Rotweiler, who ran straight towards me.

I started to scream, but Alicia told me not to worry. "Spirit just wants to get to know you," she said, "that's all."

That night we stayed up talking and eating Chinese food and ice cream, and when I went to bed I had my own room to sleep in.

The next morning, Alicia took me to the video store where she worked. There we watched videos, waited on customers, and had lunch. All she did was buy me presents all day. And she told me not to worry about anything, so I didn't.

At the end of the day we closed down the video store and went home. We saw some neighbors outside, and she introduced me to them. They were all Italian. The whole block was Italian. The neighbors were friendly people. They invited me into their house but I said no. Maybe next time. I felt like it was too soon.

About a month after living with Alicia, I got used to her and the neighborhoood. I always thought that all white people were evil, and that all they wanted to do was rape us, make fun of us, and turn us into slaves. But I was wrong.

Alicia was the nicest, sweetest, most caring, and non-judgmental white person I ever met. In fact, she was the first white person I had any real contact with. I started to love her.

I met her sister Carol, her niece Cielo, her nephew John, and her brother-in-law Sal a week after I got there. I thought they were all very nice. That night her sister Carol made fettucini alfredo for dinner. That was the first time I'd ever eaten anything like that, but it was delicious.

Alicia taught me about my black history. She taught me about Frederick Douglass and Harriet Tubman. She even taught me about Jackie Robinson, which surprised me, because I didn't think she was interested in black sports.

She taught me never to give up on myself. She taught me that no matter what anyone says about me, whether they're white or black, to just ignore them, "because people fear what they don't know." She also told me that it's not just white people who will put me down, it's black people, too.

I learned a lot from Alicia. She was very open-minded about race because she had been married to a black man. But they got a divorce. After about two years Alicia wanted to adopt me. I was now 13 and ready to be adopted.

Alicia said to me, "I love you and I want you to be my daughter." I then turned to her and said, "I love you, too. And I want you to adopt me." So we told my social worker and she said, "That's great! Except for one thing—we have to get your mother's approval first." I was kind of leery about my mother approving, but I went through with it.

My social worker finally got in contact with my mother. My mother said no. I knew she would. She said I should be with my family instead of with strangers.

I told her, "For two years nobody in my family wanted me, or they didn't have time, or they didn't have any space, but now that somebody 'nice and white' wants to claim me, you have an objection to it. It's not like you're doing anything for me."

My mother still stuck with her decision. I knew my mother didn't want me to be adopted because Alicia was white. That hurt me a lot. After everything was over with, I ended up getting ripped apart from someone who really loved and cared for me, and who I loved and cared for, too.

I was sent to live with my cousin. I didn't like it because my cousin wasn't Alicia. As soon as I got there, I started to cry. I cried like I never cried before in my life. It was a very hard and agonizing thing to deal with. I lay on the floor kicking and screaming, as I watched Alicia drive off.

After I left Alicia's home, I lost my self-esteem, I lost my energy, and I felt like I was losing my mind. I felt like everyone in the world was against me. I felt like my whole world was coming to an end.

> *I think about how my life could have been. I could have had a family who loved and cared for me.*

I often think about Alicia. I think about how my life could have been. I could have had a family who loved and cared for me. I could have had a mother who would have been there for me no matter what circumstances I had to face.

It's very unfair how so many young children and young adults have their decisions made for them. We as foster children don't really have any rights. If our biological parents aren't doing right by us, then we should have the right to say who we want to be with.

Some people feel that blacks should be with blacks and whites should be with whites. That's not true. I feel it doesn't matter what color your guardian is, so long they're doing right by you. That's all that matters.

LeFonché was 17 when she wrote this story.

Clean Slate

By Natasha Santos

I wanted a family like the happy ones on television. But chaos, fear, and lies were my life when I was living with my mother. Then, when I was 8 years old, I began my life in foster care.

Six months later my sisters and I were split up. For the next five years my foster families treated me with little respect or consideration, to say the least. The foster mother I lived with the longest, Diane, kept me in check by yelling and cursing. Then she got fed up and kicked me out. I was sent to my older sister's foster family.

My older sister was living with a "cool" family (she said). But by that time I believed in no such thing. When I arrived at her foster home I was wary. We only lived together for four months until she had to leave. Her leaving made me feel a little timid (was I next?), but I still wanted to be accepted by them.

My foster mother had a strong stubborn will, and she liked things done her way. But she didn't swear unless she was severely angry or surprised. She was quiet and didn't like a lot of trouble. I loved the way she seemed to always have just enough energy to put up with my antics. Her daughter also seemed willing to guide me when I was in crisis, even though we've had a rocky relationship.

Things were definitely better at this new home. It seemed like my foster family wanted me. And like they wanted to help me. I thought I could fit in with them, that I had found a pretty good home.

They were a real family. They stuck together and seemed to be bonded by their deep affection for one another.

I thought my new family would want to listen to me. I felt like I could tell them everything about my feelings and my past. It didn't always go well. When I talked with my mother about my past foster homes and brought up Diane's injustices, my mother always seemed to defend Diane. That hurt me. I thought she secretly agreed with how Diane treated me, and that she felt I was out of control when treated otherwise.

That made it harder for me to confide in this new family. I tried to trust them anyway, but years of rejection and ridicule had left me emotionally withdrawn. My insecurities began to appear.

It was my birthday, and I was in the house feeling alone and forgotten. No one from my biological family had called to wish me a happy birthday. So I did the only thing I felt I could do, which was to sit in my room and cry.

My foster sister came home and asked what was wrong. I refused to answer, fearful of being made fun of. She became frustrated, grabbed my diary from me, and read the newest intimate passage I had written. All I could do was stare and ask her to give it back. I felt dirty and isolated.

She looked at me afterwards and asked me if I was upset because of what I had written. I wouldn't answer. Instead of respecting my privacy, she became angry and stormed out of the room.

I felt as if she perceived the whole scene as a bid for attention, instead of my way of protecting my privacy. The rest of the family said they felt the same way at times. I was angry. How dare they judge and assume things? How dare they ridicule me?

But then there were times like Christmas and other holidays, or the rare occasions that we were all in the same room, talking and laughing together. Talking about nothing and loving it. Then I felt safe and wanted, like this is what families are about. That all the other crap that happens is just nonsense that happens in all families. That only these moments mean anything: warm feelings, a Christmas tree, and happy smiling faces. Normal family. I always wanted that.

One day it occurred to me that even normal families have conflicts, and that I had found the closest thing I'd seen so far to the families on television. I'd found what I was looking for and had better go after it. So I asked my mother if she would adopt me.

> **I thought that once I got adopted, all my past troubles would be erased. I'm still waiting for that to happen.**

My mother never actually said yes. I just kept asking her. Then, during a meeting to plan my case, I was surprised to hear my lawyer's assistant say, "Right now your long-term plan is adoption." She asked me if that was what I wanted. I said yes, nodding and acting as if I had known all along. (How very sophisticated of me!)

My mother and I went to court—after mild hesitations from me. I got dressed slowly, and had to return to the house several times because I kept forgetting "important" things.

I felt weird and uncomfortable, almost like I was to be heading for the courtroom to trade in my identity. My mother sensed my doubt and became frustrated. She said, "Come on or I'll call the entire thing off." So we went. We waited, went into the courtroom, and I was adopted. The whole thing took about 30 minutes, including the wait.

My mother and I went out to eat afterward, and I was happy just to get away from the courthouse. It felt gloomy, like it would suck up my happiness.

I thought that once I got adopted everything would change. I believed all my past troubles and trauma would be erased and that I would start new. I thought I'd feel secure in my family. I'm still waiting for that to happen.

For a long time after I got adopted, I felt angry and hurt. I still couldn't tell my family about my past without feeling like they were rejecting me. Then I gradually began to realize over the weeks, months, and years that they can't handle certain things about me, like the abuse I went through in my past.

What they did to deal with the sometimes overwhelming information I gave them was to downplay what happened. Then, when I later did something wrong or hurt them in some way, they would bring it up, as if to prove to me that what I endured wasn't abuse. Once I was late coming home on the day my new sister had to go to her grandmother's funeral. She cursed me out and threw what I had told her about the abuse back in my face, saying I shouldn't feel special.

So I've learned what to divulge and what to keep to myself. I've stopped telling them major things about myself. My feelings are spared and their minds are at rest. But trying to keep those feelings in has been a roller coaster. I still haven't dealt with my past, and it affects me.

Recently, though, I realized that I needed my mother's advice. I'd spent about six months unsuccessfully trying to figure myself out. I was asking myself, "Who am I? How does my past relate to my present? How will it relate to my future?" Thinking about things like that completely messed me up. I was upset a lot and couldn't concentrate.

During a post-Christmas morning, my mother and I discussed my mental stability. Or instability, as it were. We were incapable of doing that before, either because I feared rejection or because she feared upsetting me.

I felt anxious, but I began to tell her how I felt. I told her about my panic attacks and my paranoid thoughts about what classmates and teachers might think of me. And she listened. I told her about my struggle to forget my former life. When she listened and spoke to me understandingly and encouragingly, I was surprised.

We talked about my past foster homes, and I came to understand that maybe she wasn't defending my old foster mother, maybe she was trying to make me see that Diane had her own problems and was taking them out on me and my siblings. Realizing that was a weight-lifter, because for a long time I felt that the way Diane treated me was all my fault. I needed her to tell me it wasn't.

Lately, I think my new family has been trying harder to understand and help me. I've also begun to listen a little more closely to their feelings of frustration and anger about things I've done.

For a long time after I got adopted, I still couldn't tell my family about my past without feeling like they were rejecting me.

Once I began to listen, a lot of things started to click for me. I realized that my sisters didn't mean to hurt me with their teasing. And I understood that my mother wasn't always being distant, but was actually allowing me space to be myself. I'd rarely experienced that in other homes, where I was always told to shut up and what to think about myself.

I began to understand who they were. And by understanding, I softened my take on the whole situation. I didn't condemn them for everything they did that felt wrong. I guess we've all matured since I first arrived

It helps that I've realized that there is no such thing as a normal family, and that I will drive myself crazy looking for families like the ones on television. From hearing my friends' description of their families' embarrassing acts and arguments, it seems to me that no one always gets along. In a way, that makes me feel good. It helps me to understand that my family isn't far off from normalcy, if there is such a thing.

I came to this new home with broken spirits and a heavy heart. The poison from my former foster mothers had seeped into my soul. Now I'm getting better, I'm almost revived. I have people who want to make me well. We're learning to trust each other and to be a lot more considerate of one another. I know that, at least, I'll try. I've almost found my dream family. I want to hold on to them.

Natasha was 16 when she wrote this story. She later attended the University of New Orleans.

How Counseling Can Help You Adjust

By Tamara Scretching

Adoption can be a difficult adjustment, both for the child being adopted and for the people welcoming a new member into their family. But there are places you can go to talk about it.

The Center for Adoption Support and Education (CASE) in Maryland is a perfect example. CASE is a place where families who have adopted children can go for information and counseling. It helps both the family and child cope with problems they're having, whether right after the adoption or even years later. I spoke with Debbie Riley, executive director of CASE, to learn more.

Q: What does post-adoption counseling mean, and why is it important?

A: Post-adoption counseling can include any services provided once a child has been legally adopted into a family. Here at C.A.S.E. we have counseling sessions for families, and teen groups that bring together teens from all different kinds of adoption experiences [not just those adopted from foster care]. We also have parent groups, and workshops where younger adoptees can meet older adoptees.

It's important for children and families to have a place to talk about things like how they're adjusting, challenges around family members feeling connected to one another, identity issues related to integrating your birth family and adoptive family, and so on.

Q: Who is usually involved in the process?

A: Adoption is a family event. You don't want to just treat the adopted child in isolation. So we usually work with the whole family—the adoptive child and parents, siblings, and sometimes birth parents, depending on the relationship. But it can involve anybody whose life is touched by the adoption.

Q: What are some of the common issues that come up for kids adopted from foster care?

A: There's a lot of unresolved grief and loss, a lot of things in their lives that they are no longer connected to that they've never had the opportunity to grieve about. All adoptees, whether they were in foster care or placed [in an adoptive home] at birth, have lost connections with people, places, and things—different family members, all the schools you transferred from every time you moved during foster care, teachers, coaches, friends, and so on.

Also, a lot of kids have experienced trauma and they need to work through it. Many children who came from foster care might have grown up in situations where there's been abuse, neglect, deprivation of some kind, or moving around a lot, and those things have affected them emotionally. That means they need longer-term support to help them once they get into a stable family.

Trust is a huge issue. Often they feel adults have not been there for them, have not been trustworthy. They have a deep desire to be part of a family, but at same time they're scared to connect and attach and become dependent.

Q: What are some of the issues that parents deal with?

A: Adoptive parents are struggling, too, because they don't always know how to deal with the issues their kids are bringing. They often need help understanding the impact of trauma and neglect on their child, and learning different kinds of parenting strategies that best fit children coming from [difficult] beginnings. They need to learn how to give permission for children to talk about the past without feeling threatened by that.

Q: Do adopted teens have special counseling needs that are different from younger children?

A: Counseling needs for teens are more complicated. Most teens struggle sometime during their adolescence, but the complexities of adoption can make the task really challenging. Adolescence is a time when you try to figure out who you are and where you came from and try to learn about your identity. Adopted adolescents often have to figure this out without having a lot of information. They also have to figure this out in relationship to two sets of parents, biological and adoptive.

During adolescence you start thinking about things very differently than when you were little. So teens start thinking about why they were adopted and begin to have more questions. Sometimes they're afraid to ask, and at times people are reluctant to answer their questions because some answers are really hard and painful. They may wonder why their birth parents made certain decisions, and they sometimes worry that it was their fault.

All of these thoughts and feelings are really normal, and it's OK to talk about it with someone. They don't need to work through this all on their own.

Q: When should families get counseling, and how do you decide when it's finished?

A: Post-adoption counseling came out of a belief that adoption is a lifelong process, that it doesn't begin and end at the time of placement. What we see here at CASE is that kids and families come in at different times in their lives when they need support.

We might not see kids right when they get placed. In a lot of families it's several years after the adoption has been finalized that the families are coming back in. Often it's when the kids have reached their teen years.

Our end date is when families and children feel they are ready to leave, when they've accomplished the goals that we've set forth together.

Q: Where can you get counseling, and how can you get help paying for it?

A: The child welfare agency that handled your adoption may have information about finding someone who specializes in this kind of counseling. You can also get in touch with the North American Council on Adoptable Children (www.nacac.org). Each state has an adoption manager, too, so that's another way to track down qualified counselors and other resources.

If you can't afford to pay for counseling, you might be able to get funding from your agency, too. There are some counties and states that have set aside money for this, but it's not equal across the country.

Q: What needs to be done to increase support?

A: As an adoption community, we have to pull together and spread the word that these services are so, so important. Studies show that these services work, not only in preventing adoption failures, but in helping young people to achieve success. But these services aren't yet available everywhere. There are very few accessible centers, and many people can't afford these services. We also need more training for mental health providers, because there are not many people who specialize in this work.

Since the Adoption and Safe Families Act passed in 1997, more and more children are being adopted from foster care. But we know that children adopted from foster care are at greater risk for mental health problems, and parents need help with that. So we've got to have specialized services in place.

We're hoping that one day there may be dedicated federal funding for post-adoption services for foster children, beyond just placement, to ensure that people have a truly permanent family.

Tamara was 16 when she wrote this story.

I Lost My Brother to Adoption

By Wunika Hicks

When I was just 8 years old, I became a mother to my brother. I had to stay home all day to take care of David, who wasn't even a year old. My mother was never home. She'd be out trying to find a job, to make some money so we could have a decent meal. My father had passed away when I was 2.

So I had to do everything my mother couldn't do—make David's bottles, change his diapers (yuk!), wash him, and rock him to sleep. I'm surprised I didn't get left back because I hardly went to school. Do you know how it feels to look out the window in the morning and see other kids with their book bags while you're stuck in the house?

I really began to dislike David. I felt that if he had never been born I wouldn't have this responsibility. I felt it was his fault that I was restricted from doing the things that every young child wants to do.

So it was a relief in a way when my brother and I were placed in a foster home. I was turning 9 years old and my brother was 15 months. We were taken away because of my mother's neglect.

I didn't want to be separated from my mother. She tried so hard to keep us together. But on the other hand I was happy that I could go to school on a regular basis and play in the park with children my own age, since my foster parents would now take care of David.

Still, I hated being around my brother. I wanted him out of my sight. I treated David so badly. He wanted me to play with him or take him to the store because I had been more of a mother to him than our real mother. But although he wanted my attention I ignored him or pushed him away, because all I could see was the past, those endless days when I was stuck in the house with him.

When my foster mother saw the way I treated David, she would say to me, "One day you're going to wish you had a brother." But I didn't pay her any mind.

Eventually I moved into a new foster home. I was 13. I was hurt when I left my old foster family because I had been with them for almost five years, but the new home turned out to be much better. They treated me like their own. In the meantime, David stayed with our old foster family.

It wasn't long before my social worker told me my brother, now age 6, would be moving into a new foster home, too. But there was a twist: the social worker said that my brother's new foster parents wanted to adopt him.

When she told me this, I stood up and just walked around the room. I was in complete shock. My body was numb and I began to cry. Was this really going on? I suddenly felt so protective of David. I hadn't wanted the responsibility of being his mother, but now I didn't want anyone taking him away.

I felt it was my fault that he was being adopted. I felt the past was coming back to haunt me. I wanted David now, but when I had him I rejected him. All I could hear was my old foster mother saying, "One day you're going to wish you had a brother."

I asked my social worker if I could still see David after he was adopted. She told me that his new parents would make that decision. She also told me that they wanted to change my brother's name—not only his last name, but his first name too.

"How can they do this?" I asked the social worker. "What gives them that right? I took care of him. I'm more of a mother to him than anyone could ever be. I know what he likes and dislikes. I'm his mother, I'm his sister, I'm everything to him! I'm all the family he has—me, not some strangers!"

The social worker just looked at me. She could see the pain I was going through, but all she could say was, "That's the law."

I asked my social worker to find out if they'd allow me to see David. She said a good time for a visit would be around the Christmas vacation, if the adoptive parents agreed. I was happy that I'd finally get to see him.

> *I suddenly felt so protective of David. I hadn't wanted the responsibility of being his mother, but now I didn't want anyone taking him away.*

But before the visit could be arranged, my social worker transferred to a different department. Later I found out that the adoptive parents never even answered my request for visitation rights.

A few months later I got a new social worker, but she didn't care that I missed my brother. All she did was sit there and smoke. Pretty soon, she left too.

(I can't help but think that if I hadn't been running from social worker to social worker, I might have been able to see my brother by now. I've been in foster care for eight years and I think I've had six social workers, five law guardians, and counting.)

55

The third social worker was better. At least she listened. I told her my problems, but she told me that when my brother was adopted his records were sealed. That meant I couldn't find out where he lived, much less visit him.

I couldn't cry. The tears wouldn't come. I had cried so much that I didn't have any tears left. I felt completely alone and helpless. I had tried so hard but I hadn't gotten anywhere. I didn't have anyone who understood me.

I ran home. My foster mother asked me what was wrong and I told her how they gave me the runaround. She got in touch with my law guardian, who is looking into this matter now.

I still feel my brother's adoption is my fault. I should have been there for David when he needed me and not pushed him away. I'm a blood relative, but I turned him away when he needed me most. I could have at least showed him I loved him.

Now he's in a complete stranger's home. I haven't seen him for three years. I don't know where he lives. I don't even know his new name.

And I didn't have a chance to say goodbye. The last time I saw him—in the playroom at our agency—I didn't know it would be the last time. I walked past him without saying anything, thinking I'd see him again the next day.

> **I haven't seen my brother for three years. I don't even know his new name.**

One of the last things he said to me was, "I hate Wunika," because I had told my social worker I didn't want to see him anymore. This was when I was sick of him, just before I knew he was going to be adopted.

I think of David every day—so much that it hurts. It hurts the most when his birthday passes. He's getting older without me.

I hope he hasn't forgotten me, but remembers the times I took care of him as a mother. I don't want him to remember the times

I rejected him.

I may have pushed him away when he wanted me, but that doesn't mean I don't love him. The system didn't understand my history, my pain. They took away the only family I had. Now I don't have anyone to love.

I just hope it all works out and that I do get to see my brother one day. Wish me good luck.

---

*Wunika was 16 when she wrote this story.
She now lives in California with her two children.*

Why Do Siblings Get Separated Through Adoption?

By Wunika Hicks

I have a lot of questions about my brother's sealed adoption, so I spoke with two experts on this topic to try to get some answers: Hy Frankel, a lawyer, and Eric Brettschneider, a child welfare advocate.

Q: Why are siblings separated by adoption?
A: Sometimes it's hard to find people who want to adopt siblings instead of an individual child, and sometimes it's harder for older kids to be adopted. But the foster care system also contributes to the problem, since most children adopted in New York State come out of foster care. If brothers and sisters are not kept together in foster care, the chances increase that they will be separated if adoption occurs.

Q: Why are some adoptions sealed? Why do adoptive parents refuse visitation rights to the brother or sister of an adopted child?

A: "The [adoptive] parent has the right to decide what's best for the child. That doesn't mean that the decision is always right," said Frankel. "When parents don't allow visitation, they think they're protecting the adopted sibling. In many cases, even most cases, a better decision would be for the adoptive parent to foster a continuing sibling relationship."

Q: Do siblings have the right to visit their adopted siblings?

A: "The parents can allow it if they want," Frankel said, "but [siblings] don't have a right to it."

Q: Why do some adoptive parents change an adopted child's first and last names?

A: "Adoptive parents often try to integrate the child completely into their family and culture," Frankel said. "In my judgment, that's a mistake, particularly if that means ignoring the past sibling relationship or the child's prior identity."

How To Stay Connected

In a "sealed" or "closed" adoption, a child's records are sealed. If your sibling has been adopted in this way, you may not be able to find out where they are or how to get in touch with them.

But more and more, child welfare experts say that siblings—in most cases—should be able to stay connected both during foster care and after they're adopted. That means trying to have siblings adopted into the same family, and, if that's not possible, setting up an "open" adoption so that they can remain in contact.

If you're trying to stay connected with your siblings, it's important to know what's happening with your case and to speak up about your wants and needs. Here are a few tips.

If you and your siblings are still in foster care:

• Stand up for yourself. Caseworkers, judges, and lawyers must listen to you and consider what you want when it comes to placement and adoption. And federal law now requires agencies to make reasonable efforts to place siblings together in foster care.

• You always have the right to ask questions about your siblings, and you should. If it's not possible for you to be placed with your siblings during foster care, your agency should set up sibling visits and cover transportation costs so that you can keep in touch. If that's not happening, tell your lawyer (and the judge at your next hearing).

• If you find out that you or your siblings are being adopted, ask whether an open adoption is possible. If it's not, try to make a plan with your siblings for staying in touch. (If you have access to a computer, e-mail or MySpace can be a good way to do this.)

If you've been separated from siblings through a closed adoption:

You may still be able to reconnect. Laws vary state by state, but generally once your siblings have turned 18 (or in some states 21), you are legally entitled to search for them. Just make sure that you're emotionally ready to start that journey.

Joe Soll, director of Adoption Crossroads (a nonprofit organization for people dealing with family separation due to adoption or foster care), suggests reading up and joining a support group six months before beginning your search for family so that you are as prepared as possible for the strong emotions that can come up.

To find a support groups in your state, visit the Adoption Crossroads website at www.adoptioncrossroads.org and click on "search support sites."

For more information and resources about searching for your birth family, try the Child Welfare Information Gateway at www.childwelfare.gov/adoption/search.

---

*Wunika was 16 when she wrote this story.
She lives in California with her two children.*

Saying No to Adoption

By Akeema Lottman

For as long as I can remember, my social workers have been pressuring me into being adopted. They all say the same thing: it would best if I were to get adopted because I would have a nice loving family who cares about me. "Thousands of kids get adopted every day and they're happy," they say. "So why don't you want to be adopted?"

At 14 I got the chance to live with my first foster family. I'd been in the system for years, but I'd always lived with relatives. My social worker at the time kept telling me that this would be a nice family to adopt me because they'd adopted my younger sister at birth. But I didn't know this family, and they didn't know me. How could a social worker I barely knew determine that this was the best family for me?

But honestly, the biggest reason why I still don't want to be adopted to this day is that I don't feel like I can really trust anyone. In my experience, people have walked out of my life whenever I've started to count on them. For that reason I don't allow myself to really get close to anyone. Even though I've grown to know and love my current foster family, I still don't want to be adopted by them. I'm so used to being let down that I'm not willing to risk it.

Besides, it's natural to want to be with my own family. When I think about becoming part of a different family I feel deprived from my own life, as though I'd be losing a part of who I am. My family is a part of me. If they were taken away from me I'd feel as if I didn't have a say in my own life, like social workers were deciding who I am.

I'm getting older, and I don't want to live my life through other people's families. My sisters who have been adopted since birth carry their adopted names, and they don't really know anything about "our" family. I don't want to change my last name because then I might forget where I came from. Your last name has a history behind it, and that's something very sacred to me.

I'd rather help strengthen my own family relationships than concentrate on the connections I already have with

When I think about becoming part of a different family I feel as though I'd be losing a part of who I am.

my foster family. Many of my relatives lost themselves to drug addictions in the past, but they are now receiving help. Watching my foster family work through their problems together makes me realize that my own family doesn't support each other in that way. It reminds me that bringing my own family closer is something I've always wanted to do.

So instead of adoption, I've decided to stay in the system until

Two Moms in My Heart

I age out at 21. That way, ACS (child welfare) can help me pay my way through college and then, hopefully, I can accomplish my goals. Even though I'm choosing not to be adopted by my foster family, I really care about them. There's an important place for them in my life, but I want to focus now on my own family.

Akeema was in high school when she wrote this story.

Two Moms in My Heart

By Eric Green

One day when I was 9 years old, my foster mother, Ms. Hazel, got a call from the agency. She told my brother William and me that we were moving. Ms. Hazel then took us downtown to our agency. To our surprise, we met Lorine and Robert. They were total strangers, but they told us that they were going to adopt us. I felt a bit sad about moving, but I hoped that things would turn out well.

When I got to their house, I didn't know anything about them—who they were or where they came from. But they changed me in some good ways and made me feel like part of their family.

When I was looking like a slob, they bought me clothes. When I didn't have anything to occupy myself, they bought me video games, comic books, toys, art supplies, everything.

Soon after moving in, I drew a picture of Chun-li, a character in my videogame. I showed it to Lorine and she told me that she liked my drawing. I found out that I was an artist. I felt very welcomed and cherished. I felt happy to have a family that cared about me, and would do anything to make me feel welcome.

I decided I wanted to be adopted. I liked them and wanted a family. But as I thought about it clearly, I felt sad because I knew that adoption meant that I would never live with my biological mother, Sharon, again.

And I have found out a number of things about Lorine and Robert that make me feel a bit scared. Lorine will curse and threaten me when I get a little out of control, or, as she would say, "fresh."

When Lorine and Robert yell at me when I do something bad, I feel nervous and threatened. One time Lorine said, "If you don't shut up, I'll bash your head through the wall! And you can tell everybody in school that I said it." I felt hurt, and couldn't believe she said that. I knew she wouldn't do that. Why would she say that except to hurt me? I went to my room and started writing poems about my life.

When Lorine and I fight, I forget what she and Robert have done for me and I wish I wasn't adopted. I wish I was never in foster care and that I was still living with my biological mother, Sharon. I feel especially furious that Lorine is not like Sharon. Often I think, "If I didn't get adopted, maybe I could have lived with Sharon again. And if I was living with Sharon, I wouldn't have these problems."

I came into foster care in 1988, when I was 4 years old. Things at home were not good when I was very little. Sharon and my father, Billy, sometimes left my three siblings and me in the house for days. Times when we didn't have anything to eat, my older brother William picked food from a garbage can to feed us.

Billy was an alcoholic and, when he died, we came into foster care because Sharon was too sick to take care of us. I hoped coming into care would make things better, but it hurt to move in with parents who were not really mine. I did not want to be separated from my mother.

I felt that Sharon was my family and no one else. I also worried about her. The only friends she seemed to have were me and my siblings, David, Ebony, and William. I thought that if we were home, we could take good care of her.

When Ms. Hazel took me downtown for a family visit, Sharon would rarely show up. But when she did, I was incredibly happy that I had the chance to see her face and talk to her. I wanted the visits to go on and on.

I felt sad because I knew that adoption meant that I would never live with my biological mother again.

Whenever the visits were over, I'd feel sad. I didn't want her to leave. For me, being separated from my biological parents felt like I'd been kidnapped and taken away for a very long time.

Many times I wished that I could've gone back to live with Sharon. I'd look at other kids who had a real mother and a real father. Then, when Sharon was visiting me, I'd say to myself, "Eric, ask her if you and William can go back to live with her." But once I got adopted, I knew I was stuck with Lorine and Robert.

Even after I got adopted, I still saw Sharon a few times. On my birthday she would send me letters and even a $5 bill. And sometimes she would call to see if I was doing fine. She'd end it by saying, "I love you."

Lorine and Robert let me keep visiting Sharon. At Christmas, my oldest brother David picked up William and me and drove us to visit Sharon at her new home. We did a lot of things together, like watch TV and movies, play video games, draw, look at our pictures from when we were little, and stay up late—almost 'til morning.

Sharon could cook too! She cooked turkey, stuffing, yams, rice, and collard greens. And she even bought me Christmas presents—a racetrack set and a street fighter game.

Visiting her, we had a great time. She gave me lots of laughs, hugs, and kisses, and I called her mommy.

Four years ago, Lorine told me she had an announcement to make. She told William and me that Sharon had passed away from cancer. I felt stunned and petrified, and a tear almost came from my eye. I knew she was sick, but I didn't know she was in the hospital. I wished I could've been there for her.

I wanted to panic and say to Lorine, "How? Why did she have to go? Where did you get that information from? She shouldn't die now! It's been a long time since I visited her! Now my life is in for a rude awakening."

I felt that, when Sharon died, my world was blown to smithereens. I was shocked, surprised, sad, and confused, but mostly I was infuriated. I just wanted to do something crazy. But instead, I remained calm, relaxed, and composed. I didn't want to let on how hurt I was.

But since then, until this very moment, I have felt so mad inside because she's gone. I think about her and wish that she were alive again.

I was especially sad when I realized that our Christmas visits were over. I've thought about those memories of our family visits over and over, because those were the times when I got the chance to talk to her, to know her and to have her know me. Since then, going through the holidays without her has been the most difficult thing I've had to deal with. Moving on is not something that I have been able to do.

Lately I've been having a lot of conflicts with Lorine and Robert. I think it's partly because I'm getting older and I want more freedom, and Lorine wants me to follow all the rules she makes. But I think the bigger part of the problem is that I'm so angry and sad that Sharon is gone, and I blame Lorine for not being like her.

Not long ago, Lorine told me to come home from school and not go to the library or the pizza shop. I told her that I wouldn't go, but I lied. I don't like to be told what to do.

So that day, when school was finished, I went to the library. I stayed until it was about to close. After the library, I went to the pizza shop and bought me a slice of pizza. Then I headed home.

I was in my room settling down when Robert came and asked me, "How long have you been here?"

"I just got here."

"You just got here?" Robert asked. "Where were you?"

"I went to the library," I said, thinking angrily, "Can't a person who is intellectual go to the library? I guess not."

"You went to the library? Why did you go to the library? Didn't Lorine tell you not to go to the library?"

"Yes."

"So why did you?"

I was feeling too shy and too scared to answer his questions. Robert had a ring of keys in his right hand and I was afraid he wanted to hit me with them, even though he never has hit me. As he got direct, I stepped back in shyness.

"When Lorine tells you to listen to her, you listen to her."

Lorine jumped in and asked me, "Are you going to listen?"

I said, "Yes," so they walked out of the room, leaving me feeling nervous and shaky. Then I thought to myself, "She's not my real mother. There's no substitute for Sharon. Lorine is just someone who takes care of me."

Sometimes I love Lorine to death. But when I'm mad, I imagine that if Sharon were here she wouldn't discipline me like that. I picture a real mother as an understanding friend, someone who I can communicate with, not someone who disciplines and yells and tells me what to do.

When Lorine and Robert get mad at me, they shake their heads as if they understand me, but I think they don't. They don't know the pain and anger I feel about losing Sharon, and they don't know about the sadness and isolation I felt when I came into foster care.

Inside, I'm trying to deal with those feelings. I think I need help understanding those losses, but I won't share my feelings with Lorine and Robert because I don't trust them. If they won't listen to my feelings about getting a slice of pizza, how are they going to understand anything else about me?

Going through the holidays without her has been the most difficult thing I've had to deal with.

I know that Sharon thought it was a good idea for me to get adopted, because Lorine loves me very much and Sharon wanted Lorine to keep me and take care of me but also to help straighten out my life. Sharon told me that she thought Lorine and Robert could give me what she couldn't—good quality clothes to wear, a bed to sleep in (we all slept on one mattress when I lived with Sharon), video games to play, food to eat every day, and a good life of happiness. Sharon could only give me fun and freedom.

I believe that Sharon is in heaven watching over me now. I know she would want me to be strong and happy. She wouldn't want me to feel so angry and depressed and to be falling behind in school. She would want me to move forward in life and use my talents, like drawing. She knows that Lorine and Robert love me a lot, and wouldn't want me to go through life feeling hurt by them.

I'd like to express my feelings to Lorine. Besides fearing that she'd think my feelings were dumb, I'm afraid that, if I told her I think of Sharon as my real mother and miss her so much, Lorine might think that I don't love her, too. I also think it might be sad for Lorine if she understood that I'm going through so much pain.

Lorine has helped me feel less sad and less angry by being a good replacement for Sharon and by pushing me to do my best.

She has also told me to constantly keep in mind that Sharon still loves me. I want Lorine to help me turn my life around and make me feel happy again.

Lately, I think I've been inconsiderate toward Lorine. I've been shutting away my inner emotions and walking away angry. I've gotten into the habit of not trusting her when I do need her help.

It's affecting me not to try to trust Lorine. My sadness makes me feel like I'm losing my sense of humor. My anger makes me feel like I've lost my sense of excitement. I'll feel bad if I'm sad and angry like this for the rest of my life. Part of me is afraid of not feeling sad about Sharon. I don't want to forget the times we shared and all the memories I have of her.

If I can find the nerve, I want to ask Lorine for help in finding a way to feel happy again, without forgetting my mother.

Eric was 20 when he wrote this story.

Losing My Everything

By Jarel Melendez

When I was 17, I was sent back to live with my grandmother after seven years apart. I was thrilled, but also a little worried. I was afraid I would feel like an outsider, like I wasn't a part of the family anymore.

When the day finally came, though, stepping into my grandmother's house was like walking into heaven. My grandmother greeted my brother and me with a big hug and a kiss. She held me so long and hard it felt like my air circulation was cut off. I will never forget the first words out of her mouth: "Welcome home, baby. I missed you."

The house hadn't changed much since I left. I got my old room back, with new furniture from the agency. It was an overwhelming experience to be back home, all three of us a family again.

I was 10 when I was removed from my grandmother's house. I never understood why. When I asked my grandmother, she told me it was because the agency felt that my younger brother and I couldn't live in the same place. But in the end, we were moved back together, so that didn't make any sense. To this day I still don't know the real reason I got removed.

When it happened, I was scared to death of being away from home. I had lived with my grandmother since I was 5. I loved her, respected her, and trusted her with everything.

My grandmother was my everything because that's what she showed me. She gave me nice clothes and ironed them with starch, even if I was just going outside to play on the playground. She cooked great food for me. She made the best lasagna I ever ate in my whole life. We had some good times cooking and reading books together, and talking about any and everything.

When I was removed from my grandmother, I was put in a foster home under conditions that children shouldn't have to face. I was often hungry and cold, and I never had any money in my pockets. I was relying on my grandmother to get me through it.

My grandmother, brother, and I had scheduled visits together every two weeks. Those visits were everything to me because they let me know that I was still part of the family, that my grandmother still loved me and missed me.

She promised me that no matter what she would make every visit. But one day, a day before her next visit, my grandmother told me that she couldn't make it because my brother was sick. My heart was crushed into a million little pieces. Looking back, I know it was kind of selfish to be upset, but before that she'd never broken a promise.

Another time, my grandmother told me I was going to get a Gameboy color for Christmas. At this time Gameboy color was the must-have thing. I was so excited. Every time I talked to her she asked me what color I wanted and I told her blue. She told me, "OK, blue it is."

The day of our visit I couldn't keep myself together from the anticipation of receiving my gift. But when I got there, my grandmother told me that she could only afford to buy me some clothes for Christmas. I acted strong, but I cried for many nights. I felt that I couldn't rely on her anymore.

It was hard being in that terrible foster home without my grandmother around to help me or to talk to. I thought she would do everything in her power to make the situation better, and every little disappointment felt devastating.

Then, when I was 17, I got a new caseworker and she decided that the best place for my brother and me was back with my grandmother. After a lot of meetings, my brother and I were finally sent back to her house.

After I moved in, it seemed like I could start trusting my grandmother again. She proved herself to me by following up on things that she said she was going to do. I started thinking that maybe my expectations of her when I was in care were unreasonable. I forgave her for letting me down.

A few months later, my grandmother adopted me. I was on cloud nine. I was thrilled to be adopted because I knew that I couldn't be separated from my family again. I felt safe, because I knew that no matter what happened I had a home.

But my relationship with my grandmother wasn't like it used to be. I started noticing things about her that bothered me. For instance, her outlook on almost everything was negative.

At that time, I was graduating high school at the top of my class and working my first job. You would think she would be proud of me for doing all of that, especially after all the things I went through as a child.

But instead of saying things to encourage me, like, "Oh, wow, you are doing positive things, stay on the right track," she would say things like, "Why are you speaking like you're a white person?" and, "Why don't you hang out around the neighborhood?"

When I told her that I got an internship and was going to write about my experiences in foster care, she said, "Why would you want to talk about how messed up the foster care system is?" That was very surprising because I never heard her talk like that.

The first year after I came home I mostly excused the little comments she made. But then one day a lady from the neighborhood came up to me and told me that I seemed like a good boy, and it made no sense how my grandmother would be outside talking about me like a dog.

Another person told me the same same thing about two weeks later. My grandmother was telling people in the neighborhood that I thought I was better than everybody else, and that I kissed a lot of people's butt to get what I achieved in life.

When I first heard that I was devastated, full of anger and hurt. Most of all I felt betrayed. I never would have thought my grandmother would purposefully try to hurt me. It felt like she'd become a different person.

I never confronted her about it, mainly because I didn't want to deal with the drama that I knew she would bring to the whole situation. But I took a little time out to think back on our relationship. I remembered all the wonderful moments we had together, and the not so good ones.

> **I was thrilled to be adopted because I knew that no matter what happened, I had a home.**

Maybe she hadn't changed at all, and I just didn't realize the type of person she was when I was younger. Or maybe it's been hard for my grandma that I'm not a needy little child anymore.

By the time my grandmother adopted me I was doing so many things for myself that maybe she felt a little left out. I was working with the child welfare agency, making presentations with their speaker's bureau, and running a support group for foster teens called Circle of Youth. I was a manager at a clothing store and I'll be going to college in September. I've developed my own views of the world and become my own person, someone different from the person my grandmother is.

I think that made her feel less needed and she didn't know how to express that to me, so instead she went out and said those hurtful things.

Whatever the reason, now it seems like she really doesn't want any part of me. It really bothers me and I haven't been sure how to handle it. I'm not going to lie—there are many nights I've gone to bed and cried because I wanted her to love me and be proud of me. It is very difficult to have to change your relationship with the person that you once loved more than anything.

It's been hard for my grandma that I'm not a needy little child anymore.

I've had to change things to protect myself. Instead of talking to her about all of my business, I tell her what I want her to know. If she doesn't know something, then she can't use it against me. It hurts to have to keep some distance between us, but it is the only way we can still have a relationship.

I've learned to seek out more positive people, like case workers, friends, and neighbors, who let me know they are proud of me each and every day. It's helped me to have people around me that are there for me like she used to be.

Still, the love I have for my grandma hasn't gone away. I don't think our relationship will ever be how it was before I left to go to the foster home, and that makes me sad. But I thank her for everything that she has done for me. She will always be my grandmother.

Jarel was 20 when he wrote this story. He served as a City Year volunteer in New York City and then went to Baruch College.

Adopt-a-Teen?

By Natalie Kozakiewicz

When people think of adoption, they often think of babies or young kids getting adopted. But because of a law called the Adoption and Safe Families Act, agencies throughout the country have been trying to increase adoptions for all kids in foster care, including teens.

According to the Adoption Clearinghouse, when teens are adopted the adoption works out only about half of the time. Adoptions work out more often for younger kids, probably because it's easier for a young child to adjust to an adoptive family than it is for a teen, who already has lots of opinions that may clash with the family. But even though everyone knows that teens and kids are different, not many agencies have started treating teens differently when trying to get them adopted.

I would know. My agency tried to get me adopted when I was

14. (See my story on p. 24.) It was something they kept pressuring me to do. They took pictures of me and put them in a book as if I were a product they were trying to sell. To make things worse, I didn't even know if I wanted to be adopted.

Eventually my agency found me a family. The family seemed wonderful, but I only met up with them a few times before I was supposed to decide if they should adopt me or not. I felt like the family was rushing the process, as if they were trying to buy my sister and me by giving us things like jewelry. There was a lot of pressure and confusion for me to decide what to do. In the end, I decided not to be adopted.

Adoptions work out more often for younger kids, probably because it's easier for them to adjust than it is for a teen

But some teens do have good experiences with adoption. Chris, who I interviewed, is one of them. He was in foster care since he was 1, living with his uncle and his uncle's wife. When he was a teen, his uncle's wife adopted him. It didn't feel strange to Chris to be adopted by her, because he had known her since he was practically born. And he didn't have to go through the process of taking pictures and having strangers decide whether they wanted to be his new parents, and whether he wanted to be their son.

To find out whether Chris' or my experience was more typical of teens who are up for adoption, I talked to a man named Pat O'Brien who works for an agency in New York City called "You Gotta Believe!" His agency works to get teens adopted. O'Brien says that his agency is really a homeless prevention program, since he tries to get teens homes before they age out of care without a family to fall back on and end up on the streets. I think that's a great thing.

O'Brien agrees that agencies need to go about adopting teens differently than they do younger kids. He says that his agency first finds families for teens by looking to see what people are already in the teens' lives who might adopt them. That's the way Chris got adopted. I think this is a good way to adopt teens, who will feel better in a home where they already know someone, and who might not trust that strangers who are acting nice and caring will keep being nice and caring when you live with them.

But sometimes O'Brien puts teens on his TV show to try to find adoptive homes for them. If a child is young and doesn't have anyone in their lives, I think it is all right to try to get them adopted by putting them on TV. The child probably won't realize what's happening, and won't feel badly.

But to be a teen and have your picture on TV is not cool. I would never want my picture to be on TV. I would feel like a product, and what if people from school or where I live saw me? I would be embarrassed and ashamed.

I think it's a good idea that agencies are trying to give teens the chance to be adopted, but they need to realize that teens are not kids and will feel bad if they're being marketed like a product. I believe the teens should be able to spend lots of time with a family to see if adoption is the right thing. This could help teens feel better about being adopted, and help prevent adoptions that don't work out.

Natalie was 16 when she wrote this story. She later went to college and graduate school, majoring in anthropology.

Looking for a Mother Who Won't Leave

By Lishoné Bowsky

I was 2 years old when I went into foster care, and 7 when I got adopted. Not long after that, my biological mom stopped visiting me with no explanation. Even though those changes happened when I was so young, I think they've affected me to this day.

For years I wanted to find my biological mother. I used to cry just thinking of her at night. I missed her so much. As I got older, I wanted to live with her and be close. I used to think about her every day. I always wondered if she loved me, and why she didn't stick by my side.

I also never felt 100% sure of my adoptive mom's love. When we argued, I thought she might leave me. I really wanted both of my moms to prove their love to me.

But when I started to act up as a teenager, they proved me

wrong instead. They proved that they had an easy way of giving up on me. And that hurt.

Trouble started with my adoptive mom when I was 13 years old. We went to Puerto Rico on vacation. I enjoyed hanging out with my friends, mostly older guys and a couple of girls. But then rumors spread about me having sex with different guys.

The rumor got to my mother and she believed it. I felt mad and upset. How could she believe that? Every time I tried to explain that those guys were just friends, she wouldn't listen.

I was so hurt that she wouldn't listen to what I said that after a few days I gave up on trying to get her to believe me. I felt like she gave up on me, and because I never felt sure of her love, I took it really hard. I thought she was just another mother rejecting me.

After that, I started coming home late every day. I guess I wanted to test my mother's love. But she just got mad and threatened to call the cops. The way she treated me made me hate her.

Even after we got back to New York, I felt angry. I tried to deal with my anger by finding someone else to love me. In the winter I met this guy I really liked and I started cutting school, drinking, smoking weed and cigarettes, hanging out with gang members, and going to parties. I knew it was wrong, but I still followed him everywhere he went and came home really late.

For years I wanted to find my biological mother. I used to cry just thinking of her at night.

My relationship with my adoptive mom got rough. She wanted me home after school every day. I said that I hated being stuck at home and that my friends could do what they wanted, so why couldn't I? She'd say that she was the adult and I was the child, and I had to listen to her for my own good.

Then one night I came home around midnight. My adoptive mother didn't let me in the house. I overheard her talking on the phone, telling the police what was going on. I wanted to run away, but I had nowhere to go. So I stayed in the hallway feeling scared and wondering, "What will the cops do to me?" Fifteen minutes later they were knocking on my mother's door with me standing beside them.

My adoptive mother explained that she couldn't have me coming home late because she was getting too old for it. I felt sad for her and I understood why she thought I was too much to handle. But I also hated her for giving up on me.

The cops told me to get a sweater. Next thing I knew I was in handcuffs, heading out to their car. They took me to the foster care system. I was scared.

The next morning I went to court. The judge asked me what I was doing wrong. I told her I was coming home late, drinking, smoking, disobeying my mom, and hanging around with different people. The judge didn't ask why I was doing these things and I didn't tell her. (If she did ask, I don't think I would've trusted her anyway.) She just put me in the system and I went to a group home in the Bronx.

Going into the system felt really bad. I wanted to be in my adoptive mother's house. I got homesick and thought, "Oh my god, I'm stuck here. I'm never going home."

At first I felt guilty because I knew I messed up. But then I started to get upset. My adoptive mom didn't call me. When I visited her she acted joyful and happy to see me, but she didn't say anything about what happened between us. I wanted her to say, "I'm sorry." When she didn't, I felt she betrayed me. I told myself, "It's OK. I don't care. I'll get over it." I didn't tell her how I felt, because I felt sure that she didn't care.

I was only at the group home for a month before I gave up staying there. I started AWOLing to my boyfriend's house. Then his family got tired of me being there every day, so my boyfriend and I stayed in the streets for a while.

It was a rough time being in the streets. I felt dirty, nasty, poor, and like a bum. It hurt me very much to be kicked out of my biological family, my adoptive family, and his family. I also felt bad that I stopped going to school. I never thought I would live in the streets and stop going to school.

After a while I decided to find my biological mother, because I thought she could get me out of the system and I wanted to get to know her. When I was younger, my adoptive mom had a picture of my bio-mom and my father and she would show it to me when I asked to see it. I still remembered that picture. I wanted to know everything about her. I wanted her to prove that she loved me after all.

I asked my adopted mother for my biological mother's old address.

She understood that I wanted to learn more about my biological mom, so she gave it to me and said, "Good luck finding her."

I was nervous, though, because I feared she wasn't going to want to know me. I thought she might still be on drugs and prostituting, and that she would deny having me. Luckily, that's not how it went.

When I finally found her I cried and cried. So did she. They were happy tears because that was the first time in seven years that I got to hold her in my arms.

> **I asked my adopted mother for my biological mother's old address. She gave it to me and said, "Good luck finding her."**

I thought my bio-mom was nice, funny, beautiful, confident, and determined. We looked a lot alike and seemed similar in our mentality: we go for what we want, and if we can't get it at first we still try.

I moved in with her and we went to the movies together and talked about when I was a baby, before her drug use made me end up in care. We traveled to see all of our family together. I felt like I'd come home. I loved starting to understand who she is and why she couldn't take care of me when I was little. Finding that out from her was a relief. And when she told me she couldn't get me out of the system because her rights to me were terminated, I cried.

Two Moms in My Heart

I got used to being with her and her boyfriend so much that I started calling her "mom" and her boyfriend my stepfather. I thought I finally had everything I wanted, but things didn't stay that way for long. A couple months after I found her, my biological mother found a new boyfriend and broke up with my stepfather, who I felt close to. That was very upsetting.

Then my mom and I had a fight because her new boyfriend took his attitude out on her and I hated it. So I told my biological mother I didn't like it. She told me to mind my business. I got mad and pushed her. She pushed me back and I fell on my bed. I got so mad I punched her. We fought.

That night my biological mother decided to throw me out. She told me I had to go in the morning and take all my stuff with me. I said that was no problem. The next day, I packed my stuff and left.

I felt so confused and angry that day. It felt weird fighting my own mother. And I felt guilty, like I had messed up because I didn't listen to her.

I also felt like my bio-mom let me down, though, because she threw me out for her boyfriend. That hurt me a lot.

When I think about my bio-mom now, a lot of stuff scrambles through my mind, but I can't get my thoughts to settle down so I can figure out where things went wrong between us.

Now I'm in a residential treatment program, and even though I'm separated from everyone I care about, I do still talk to my biological and adoptive mothers and see them sometimes. My adoptive mom shows me she cares by coming to some meetings or court dates. Sometimes we strike up a conversation.

I love and will always have a lot of love for my adoptive mother. I'd like to tell her my side of the story—that I felt hurt that she believed the rumors about me, but that I also didn't want to leave her home. I'd also like to give her a hug, tell her "I love you," and talk more often.

My biological mom also tells me "I love you" and sometimes

visits or talks to me on the phone. I'm happy that she's back in my life. I'd like to tell her that I love her and understand all the things she has been through. I hope that she can forget about the past and move on so we can be close.

But right now I don't feel ready to tell my two moms that I love them. I feel scared to do that. Maybe I still don't trust that they love me back. I hope that my mothers will stay in touch with me and show me that I can trust them. Then maybe I'll be able to let them know that how I acted didn't always show what I was really feeling.

Lishoné was 23 when she wrote this story. She has since had a daughter and earned a graduate degree in public policy.

Adoptive Families Need Support

By Lishoné Bowsky

If you're lucky, being adopted means that you've found yourself a nice home with people who care about you and adopted you because they love you.

But even with the most loving families, being adopted often leaves a child to deal with feelings of loss, abandonment, and rejection—feelings felt not just in childhood but during your teenage years as well.

"Adopted children sometimes have more of a difficult adolescence, when they're trying to figure out who they're going to be," said Maris Blechner, one of the founders of Family Focus, an agency that gets older children and children with special needs adopted.

Because they're often dealing with more confusion and hurt

than other kids, when they hit their teens, kids who are adopted sometimes act out, get in trouble, and fight with their parents. Sometimes things get very tense. Parents even sometimes send their kids to military school, Blechner said, or to live with relatives.

Adoptive families often need support to cope with the difficult times—like individual and group counseling. But "there's a big missing part, a giant gaping hole in post-adoption services," said Blechner. "One agency does some, others don't."

Unlike a lot of agencies, Blechner's agency tells their families who adopt, "We will be there for you for the rest of your life." Sometimes that help can be with the small things—like if they move and their subsidy checks stop coming (parents of kids who are adopted often receive checks just like foster parents do) or if they can't get a copy of the birth certificate.

Or it can be with the big emotional issues—like the case of one woman who recently called about her 15-year-old son who was getting into lots of trouble.

"Help me," she said. "He's driving me crazy. I must have done something wrong."

People from Blechner's agency are now meeting with the woman, talking her through some of her difficulties, and helping her and her son find counselors to talk to.

Looking back at my own adoption, I realize that my family's support system wasn't as strong as it could have been, especially during my teenage years, when I was trying to find myself and starting to rebel. I was involved in lots of activities in and out of school, which surrounded me with people. But I felt like those people judged me and saw me as an outsider because I was adopted.

Maybe my adoption could have been better had I attended a group for kids who had been adopted. I would have felt that we all had being adopted in common.

Blechner agrees with me. She said it can help for adopted

kids to talk to other adopted kids.

"Teens deserve to be able to sit down with other adoptive kids without adults around," she added. This way they can say whatever it is they feel without having to worry about hurting their parents' feelings and feeling guilty about it later on. And they can see that the feelings they might have about adoption—like that they don't really belong or that they're unlovable—aren't strange and that other adoptive teens have them too.

> **Even with the most loving families, being adopted often leaves a child to deal with feelings of loss, abandonment, and rejection.**

Blechner also said adoptive parents need support.

"Raising adoptive kids is not the same [as raising biological children]. It requires more sensitivity, special understanding, flexibility. You may need to be more open to the outside world and [seek out] places to go for help."

But according to Blechner, help is exactly what there's not enough of in too many places. Too many agencies say, "Here's your kid, now you're on your own."

When parents are given a child to adopt, it is a lifetime commitment.

Lishoné was 19 when she wrote this story.
She went on to earn a graduate degree in public policy.

More Than Love

By Kathy Dugan

Kathy Dugan is the mother of 12 children, eight of whom she and her husband adopted from foster care. When she first adopted in the late 1970s, Dugan discovered that very few therapists understood the needs of adopted kids and their families. Dugan founded the Center for Adoption Support and Education so that adoptive families would have access to information and the specialized services that she had needed but couldn't get. Kathy describes her early struggles raising adopted kids with special needs.

In the beginning, I would sometimes think, "Who could know how to parent better than me?" I already had four children of my own when I first adopted. But I found out I had a lot to learn.

Later there were times when I wondered if I actually knew anything about parenting. And trying to find someone with expertise, not just about adoption but about foster care, was like walking down a road blindfolded.

Some of my adopted children were abused physically and sexually, and three have fetal alcohol effect. But when I started adopting 30 years ago, there was no such [diagnosis] as fetal alcohol effect or syndrome. I'd have psychologists and psychiatrists telling me things like, "Their elevator just isn't stopping on every floor."

It was so unprofessional. Most of the therapists were clueless. Everyone seemed to think that if a child just had a roof over its head and a loving family, if you took care of them and you unconditionally loved them the way you'd love any child you had, that's all they needed.

I just knew my kids needed something more than me just loving them. It was very frustrating, but I just kept at it, talking to another person and another and another. I learned something from every single therapist I went to.

I had great disappointment on two levels: disappointment that I wasn't parenting these children the way they needed to be parented, and also watching them make such poor decisions that were almost certainly going to impact their lives forever.

I also had a great deal of sadness. My adopted kids would say all these painful things when they were small, and I'd think they were getting over those things little by little as I saw them doing well in school, making friends, loving sports—all the things kids do where you can see their self-esteem growing. Then I'd realize that all the negative messages they'd received in the past from birth parents or other people were still echoing through their minds. There was part of them that continued to believe that those negative messages were true.

It's a helpless feeling as a parent not to be able to reverse that thinking. You feel inadequate. You're always explaining yourself to teachers because of inappropriate behaviors, spending so much time in the counseling office at school.

I learned pretty quickly that my friends and family weren't really in the arena I needed them to be in. People would say things like, "What did you expect when you adopted children whose backgrounds you didn't know much about?" That wasn't helpful.

One thing that really helped me was getting individual counseling. That helped me think about my motivations and whether I was being realistic about my expectations. These are the things you don't really have a lot of time to think about when you're caught up in everyday life.

I already had four children of my own when I first adopted. But I found out I had a lot to learn.

Another helpful thing, which I didn't have at first, was a support group. I eventually linked up with other parents and we started our own support group without realizing that's what it was. That was so helpful to me on many levels.

Support groups are phenomenal for helping you work through the frustration of thinking you're doing the right thing and having it blow up in your face. I didn't feel like such a loser, and I began realizing that it really had so little to do with parenting skills. I never gave up. I just kept thinking, "There has to be something more for these children."

Embracing My Daughter's Children

By Bevanjae Kelley

My daughter was only 17 when she had her first child, Michelle.

At the time, Nicole was still suffering from the trauma she had gone through five years before. At age 12, she was kidnapped and sexually assaulted. It happened one morning after she walked her little brother to school, when I was out at a job interview. This had a devastating impact on her life and mine. She became rebellious and sexually promiscuous, and I felt helpless, guilty and angry.

Still, for the first year after Michelle was born, Nicole acted like a new mother. While she was not necessarily doting, she was caring and tried her best.

Then my husband died following a long illness. We were all in pain and feeling vulnerable. My daughter had been the apple of her father's eye—until her mid-teens they would go on camping outings, he would take her shopping, or they'd go bowling and to the movies. I believe she was the most devastated when he died.

A year after that, Nicole gave birth to her second child, Danielle, and then moved out with her daughters. For a long time already she'd been drinking and smoking weed, but once she moved, it started to affect her parenting. She began leaving her children with strangers and not coming back to pick them up for a few days. Or she'd smoke weed and drink until she passed out in a deep sleep, unaware of what her children were doing. Once when I was there, Michelle was hungry and I saw her try to eat the cat food.

All of these things made me angry, scared, and ashamed. I thought of myself as a caring and nurturing mother, but somehow I failed my daughter. How could I have raised a daughter who would neglect her own children? I blamed myself for Nicole's behavior.

I tried to empathize. I knew that Nicole wasn't a whole person. She was still grieving from her injuries and the death of her father. But even when I tried to help, Nicole took my actions as criticism, a personal assault, like I was the enemy in a war between us.

It was not easy for me to become a parent again. It's still just as exhausting, physically and emotionally.

When she rejected me, she made me feel like I meant nothing to her, like I was a nobody in the street. I felt so frustrated and sad. All I wanted was for her to snap out of it!

Since I couldn't seem to help her, over the next few months I began to stay away from my daughter more and more. I traveled a lot, visiting my siblings and mother, dealing with my own grief and focusing on my son.

Then one night I received a call from my daughter, crying, "They took my kids, Ma! I don't know where they took them!"

"Who?"

"ACS and the police."

When the New York City foster care system, ACS, came into her life, Nicole and I talked about what to do. She agreed to voluntarily give her children to the agency only if I took them.

As the investigation dragged on, my daughter agreed to let the judge terminate her parental rights. Then I adopted her two children. We discussed that she would still be in their lives and that she could get herself together and take them back. Although she was legally not their mom anymore, we agreed that we would find a way for them to be back together.

When they came into my care, Michelle was almost 4 and Danielle was 14 months. Now they're 11 and 8. I can't believe I've had them seven years.

It was not easy for me to become a parent again. I thought as they got older it would be easier, but it's still just as exhausting, physically and emotionally.

Even so, I embraced her children as my daughters. I put Michelle into pre-K, potty trained Danielle, and weaned her from the bottle. From the beginning Danielle had a warm, affectionate, happy disposition. Michelle, on the other hand, acted stubborn and angry and threw tantrums. Michelle had lived with her mother for longer, and she missed her more.

At the time I took her daughters, I think Nicole was relieved. She was definitely overwhelmed by the responsibility of caring for her two small girls. But I think that my daughter also felt ashamed and alone when she lost her kids. The first few years that my granddaughters lived with me, my daughter had very little contact with us. She would talk to her kids on the phone and make plans to see them, but wouldn't keep her word.

I found out later that she had formed a close relationship with the family of her new boyfriend, and she eventually had two more girls with him. It was very hard for me when I didn't know where Nicole was or how she was doing. I don't think she knew how to handle our relationship either.

One day when she visited I noticed she'd put on weight, but she didn't tell me she was pregnant. The next time she came, she put a baby carrier down in the living room and asked me, "Do you think you'll like your new granddaughter?" I was very angry at Nicole for how she was treating her daughters and me. That time in our lives felt very strange and out of control.

Looking back on my relationship with my daughter is sometimes hard for me. It's easier for me to focus on our lives now, because things are finally getting better for her and me.

Nicole became serious about turning her life around after she spent a short time in jail. She said that she never wanted to be locked up again, and since then she has truly grown into a wonderful woman and parent. She finished a training program that helped her get her life together. Since then she has been working at a government agency for almost two years and has moved into an apartment of her own.

With the two daughters she has at home, Nicole makes sure they get to school on time, do all their homework, go to bed on time, and respect their peers as well as adults. She makes them her priority.

At the time I took her daughters, I think Nicole was relieved.

It gives me great pride to know that my daughter has come a long way in the last three years. I feel that we are getting over most of the hurdles. We are more loving toward each other and respectful.

It helps that, through years of individual and family therapy, I have been able to give myself permission to forgive myself for not being able to heal my daughter. I think my daughter has forgiven me, too.

I've also changed my style of parenting with Nicole's daughters. I've been more patient and shown more affection by hugging and praising my granddaughters. I'm proud of how I've changed, and I think Nicole is proud of me, too.

Two Moms in My Heart

Every weekend Nicole either visits the girls at my home, or the girls stay with her. Having more contact with their mother means so much to them, especially Michelle. The visits and therapy have helped Michelle become less aggressive and worrisome. She even laughs a little more.

There are some things that I will never know or understand about my daughter, but I'm so glad that she has reached out to me again. She is asking my advice, and she recently became engaged and asked me to be part of planning her wedding reception. I gladly accepted.

Although I don't know what the future holds for us, my daughter and I know that we are family.

Bevanjae works to help parents in the child welfare system as a parent advocate at the Child Welfare Organizing Project.

A Family to Raise Her

By Jennifer Jeanne Olensky

It was as if all the glory of heaven was shining down, into my heart. In her eyes I learned the true meaning of love, in her presence the feeling of complete tranquility. This tiny miracle was the most beautiful child I had ever seen.

I cannot believe it has been 11 years since I said goodbye to my daughter. As I sit here looking at her picture, I think about how it all happened and what led me to the choices I made.

My father had always made me feel like "Daddy's little girl," showering me with love. But when I was 5, my parents separated. Shortly after my 13th birthday, I went to live with my father.

At the time, I believed my father's absence was my mother's doing, and I embedded a hatred in my heart for her. I spent that time building my father up in my imagination. He was a king to me—he could do no wrong. When I arrived at Daddy's, I thought

Two Moms in My Heart

I had what I had wanted for so long.

I was wrong. My Daddy loved me—he told me so every day. The only problem was his need for pills and heroin. Often we did not have food to eat. Eventually he began beating me. He would punch me in the head and knock me to the ground. As I lay on the floor waiting for him to finish, he would kick me in the back of the head and legs. Several times I thought I would die. By the morning he never remembered.

I knew I had to leave, but I really had nowhere to go. My mother would hang up the phone upon hearing my voice, so I turned to my boyfriend, Alex. I was 14, he was 18. He snuck me into his house some nights. Not wanting to get him in trouble with his family, I would often sleep in his car.

Alex was all I had. He told me he loved me and I believed I loved him. For three months I clung to him for my life. Then the police picked me up. They brought me to a Catholic group home for girls. After my first physical, I was sent to Rosalie Hall, a home for pregnant teens. That was the way I learned that I was pregnant.

When I told Alex, he said that if I didn't get an abortion, he was washing his hands of the whole situation.

But I never even considered abortion. I wanted a family. At the time I had no one, and I guess I needed something to hold onto. When Alex told me he wanted nothing to do with a baby, I was upset but also in denial. I didn't believe that he would be so cold. I thought eventually he'd come around...but he didn't.

The 30 other girls in Rosalie Hall welcomed me, along with the aides, the teachers, counselors, cleaning lady, and even the cook. They tried to be like family, but they were not. I had lost everything. I felt alone and scared.

Alex still insisted he loved me, which gave me something to hold onto. He kept in touch until I was about three months pregnant. Then he told me he couldn't continue to be in touch. He said it was only because he was pretending to see this other girl so that his family wouldn't find out I was pregnant with his baby. I was foolish enough to believe him.

For the next two months, I thought mainly about Alex. But after not hearing from him for all that time, I began thinking about my baby. The more I thought about it, the more I knew I needed to give my child a good life. The hardest part was realizing I could not. I was alone in the foster care system, but I wanted my child to have a loving, supportive environment with a mother and a father.

At five months, I decided to give up my child for adoption.

Once again I felt all alone and knew, without a doubt, that my decision to give my child up for adoption was right.

I told my counselor, Stephanie. We spoke about it several times. I knew deep within that it was right, but I decided not to tell anyone else. I knew the other girls would ridicule me, and the decision was hard enough already.

During the last few months of my pregnancy, Alex visited once and called twice. Each time he proclaimed his love for me. I believed all he said. I guess I needed to believe. Like with my father, in my eyes Alex could do no wrong. I spent every waking moment listening for the phone to ring, wishing he would call. Most nights I cried myself to sleep.

Instead of Alex, it was my father who eventually called. When I heard his voice on the phone, I was scared. He didn't know about my pregnancy. I was also happy. I loved him regardless of what he had done. He said, "Baby, I have something to tell you. I need to come see you."

My heart sank. I said, "Daddy, if you are coming to see me, I have to tell you something. I live in a group home for pregnant girls."

"You schmuck!" he yelled.

"Daddy, I don't need you to yell at me. If you can't be there for me, I am going to hang up the phone."

"I'm sorry, baby," He paused for a moment and said, "I'm

dying. I have AIDS."

My head started spinning, a lump formed in my throat. AIDS was like the Black Plague at the time. No one understood it.

I couldn't handle this, not now. I couldn't let my father hear me cry. I quickly hung up, claiming I had to go. But eventually my father came to see me. He had gotten clean of drugs, and for the next few months I spent quality time with him. He picked me up and took me out, respecting my decision about the adoption, just loving me.

But a month before the baby was due he left for Florida. There were relatives with whom he needed to make his peace.

Once again I felt all alone and knew, without a doubt, that my decision to give my child up for adoption was right. How could I allow a child to be subjected to the pit I had found myself in, abandoned by everyone I loved, and all those who claimed to love me?

When I was seven months pregnant I met Ann, a social worker with the adoption agency. She came to visit me several times. I told her I wanted my baby to have a good life. She did her best to assure me that everything would be fine.

Ann presented me with files of different families. Eventually I chose a couple who had been together several years, she a college professor, he a lawyer. From their file, I felt confident that they had a strong sense of family, with a marriage built on mutual love and respect. I knew they were the ones.

On September 28, my labor started. On September 29, I arrived at the hospital at 9:30 p.m. I was alone, scared, and in a world of pain. Looking back with the faith I have now, I believe God was with me, not only in those final hours of my pregnancy, but every step of the way. I cannot understand where all my strength and energy came from if not from God.

On September 30, at 1:46 a.m., I looked into my daughter's eyes, and love, joy, and happiness overwhelmed me. In the midst of all life's tragedies my heart was singing. For the first time in my life I felt true love. Over the next two days, I spent every possible moment with her. I never wanted to forget. I never wanted that feeling to fade.

Ann was supposed to pick her up on the third day. I was not ready to let go. I asked for three more days. Ann was reluctant at first, but gave in.

The evening before I was released from the hospital, Alex came to see us. I had called to inform him of her birth. I suppose he wanted to satisfy his curiosity. He held her and fed her. When he said goodbye, he left in tears, never voicing his feelings. It was devastating. Part of me wanted him to say, "OK, we're going to keep her!" But I knew it wouldn't happen.

For the next few days after I left the hospital, I walked over about four times a day to see my baby. She was extremely quiet, I never heard her cry. She would let out a small noise, then put her fingers in her mouth. She fussed a little when hungry, but as soon as she heard my voice, she became very quiet and alert.

Only a few days and I felt so connected. "How can I do this?" I thought. I asked Stephanie what would happen if I changed my mind.

"Foster care," was her response. "You did not apply for mother-child placement. There are waiting lists."

I thought about it and knew it would be wrong. She deserved an immediate warm, loving environment, not the uncertainty I would face. Besides, I wanted her to have a permanent, stable home, and that was something I knew at the time I couldn't provide.

The morning Ann came to get her, I had time for one feeding. As I held her, I spoke to her, studied, rocked, and hugged her. After some time I settled her into the bassinet and rubbed her back as she fell asleep. Kissing her head, I said goodbye. It was so hard to leave. I began to feel numb, just going through the motions, trying to stay strong.

Then we went to Stephanie's office with Ann and Sister Diane, and I was presented with adoption papers. As they were explained to me, I sobbed, unable to stop. Sister Diane said, "That's it! I will not notarize these papers. You are keeping your baby." Then Ann put the pen in my hand. That shocked me, and suddenly I stopped crying and signed the papers. I quietly walked back to my room and stared at the wall.

> **"How can I do this?" I thought. I asked Stephanie what would happen if I changed my mind.**

I don't remember much of what happened over the next several days. As I slowly resurfaced, I thought and thought. The most important thing I thought about was them—the couple, my daughter's parents. Instead of thinking about my loss, I was able to imagine their joy as they set their eyes upon their child. I shared in their happiness, and trusted that they would take this truly amazing gift and nurture her, love her.

Like I said, all of this happened 11 years ago, when I was 14. Now I'm 25. I have some pictures, and a five-page letter her parents sent me. In their letter, my daughter's parents said that I was their angel sent from heaven, that I was a special person with the capacity to love in a special way. They believed I had a wonderful future ahead, and that God always provides a time to be happy.

I also sent a letter to them and one for our daughter when she is older. I know I will see her one day, and hope to develop a relationship then.

I know they are special people and that our daughter was the angel heaven sent. My future looks great, and God really does provide a time to be happy.

I did what was right and do not regret it. In giving her up, I gave two loving people the family they longed for, my daughter the chance to thrive, and myself the chance to grow, to become the person I am now. I think of her on a regular basis and she is a part of me. Although I cannot see her, the love for her in my heart continues to grow.

FICTION SPECIAL

Lost and Found

Darcy Wills winced at the loud rap music coming from her sister's room.

My rhymes were rockin'
MC's were droppin'
People shoutin' and hip-hoppin'
Step to me and you'll be inferior
'Cause I'm your lyrical superior.

Darcy went to Grandma's room. The darkened room smelled of lilac perfume, Grandma's favorite, but since her stroke Grandma did not notice it, or much of anything.

"Bye, Grandma," Darcy whispered from the doorway. "I'm going to school now."

Just then, the music from Jamee's room cut off, and Jamee rushed into the hallway.

The teen characters in the Bluford novels, a fiction series by Townsend Press, struggle with many of the same difficult issues as the writers in this book. Here's the first chapter from *Lost and Found*, by Anne Schraff, the first book in the series. In this novel, high school sophomore Darcy contends with the return of her long-absent father, the troubling behavior of her younger sister Jamee, and the beginning of her first relationship.

"Like she even hears you," Jamee said as she passed Darcy. Just two years younger than Darcy, Jamee was in eighth grade, though she looked older.

"It's still nice to talk to her. Sometimes she understands. You want to pretend she's not here or something?"

"She's not," Jamee said, grabbing her backpack.

"Did you study for your math test?" Darcy asked. Mom was an emergency room nurse who worked rotating shifts. Most of the time, Mom was too tired to pay much attention to the girls' schoolwork. So Darcy tried to keep track of Jamee.

"Mind your own business," Jamee snapped.

"You got two D's on your last report card," Darcy scolded. "You wanna flunk?" Darcy did not want to sound like a nagging parent, but Jamee wasn't doing her best. Maybe she couldn't make A's like Darcy, but she could do better.

Jamee stomped out of the apartment, slamming the door behind her. "Mom's trying to get some rest!" Darcy yelled. "Do you have to be so selfish?" But Jamee was already gone, and the apartment was suddenly quiet.

Darcy loved her sister. Once, they had been good friends. But now all Jamee cared about was her new group of rowdy friends. They leaned on cars outside of school and turned up rap music on their boom boxes until the street seemed to tremble like an earthquake. Jamee had even stopped hanging out with her old friend Alisha Wrobel, something she used to do every weekend.

Darcy went back into the living room, where her mother sat in the recliner sipping coffee. "I'll be home at 2:30, Mom," Darcy said. Mom smiled faintly. She was tired, always tired. And lately she was worried too. The hospital where she worked was cutting staff. It seemed each day fewer people were expected to do more work. It was like trying to climb a mountain that keeps getting taller as you go. Mom was forty-four, but just yesterday she said, "I'm like an old car that's run out of warranty, baby. You know what happens then. Old car is ready for the junk heap. Well, maybe that hospital is gonna tell me one of these days—'Mattie Mae Wills, we don't need you anymore. We can get somebody younger and cheaper.'"

"Mom, you're not old at all," Darcy had said, but they were only words, empty words. They could not erase the dark, weary lines from beneath her mother's eyes.

Darcy headed down the street toward Bluford High School. It was not a terrible neighborhood they lived in; it just was not good. Many front yards were not cared for. Debris—fast food wrappers, plastic bags, old newspapers—blew around and piled against fences and curbs. Darcy hated that. Sometimes she and other kids from school spent Saturday mornings cleaning up, but it seemed a losing battle. Now, as she walked, she tried to focus on small spots of beauty along the way. Mrs. Walker's pink and white roses bobbed proudly in the morning breeze. The Hustons' rock garden was carefully designed around a wooden windmill.

As she neared Bluford, Darcy thought about the science project that her biology teacher, Ms. Reed, was assigning. Darcy was doing hers on tidal pools. She was looking forward to visiting a real tidal pool, taking pictures, and doing research. Today, Ms. Reed would be dividing the students into teams of two. Darcy wanted to be paired with her close friend, Brisana Meeks. They were both excellent students, a cut above most kids at Bluford, Darcy thought.

"Today, we are forming project teams so that each student can gain something valuable from the other," Ms. Reed said as Darcy sat at her desk. Ms. Reed was a tall, stately woman who reminded Darcy of the Statue of Liberty. She would have been a perfect model for the statue if Lady Liberty had been a black woman. She never would have been called pretty, but it was possible she might have been called a handsome woman. "For this assignment, each of you will be working with someone you've never worked with before."

Darcy was worried. If she was not teamed with Brisana,

maybe she would be teamed with some really dumb student who would pull her down. Darcy was a little ashamed of herself for thinking that way. Grandma used to say that all flowers are equal, but different. The simple daisy was just as lovely as the prize rose. But still Darcy did not want to be paired with some weak partner who would lower her grade.

"Darcy Wills will be teamed with Tarah Carson," Ms. Reed announced.

Darcy gasped. Not Tarah! Not that big, chunky girl with the brassy voice who squeezed herself into tight skirts and wore lime green or hot pink satin tops and cheap jewelry. Not Tarah who hung out with Cooper Hodden, that loser who was barely hanging on to his football eligibility. Darcy had heard that Cooper had been left back once or twice and even got his driver's license as a sophomore. Darcy's face felt hot with anger. Why was Ms. Reed doing this?

Hakeem Randall, a handsome, shy boy who sat in the back row, was teamed with the class blabbermouth, LaShawn Appleby. Darcy had a secret crush on Hakeem since freshman year. So far she had only shared this with her diary, never with another living soul.

It was almost as though Ms. Reed was playing some devilish game. Darcy glanced at Tarah, who was smiling broadly. Tarah had an enormous smile, and her teeth contrasted harshly with her dark red lipstick. "Great," Darcy muttered under her breath.

Ms. Reed ord e red the teams to meet so they could begin to plan their projects.

As she sat down by Tarah, Darcy was instantly sickened by a syrupy-sweet odor.

She must have doused herself with cheap perfume this morning , Darcy thought.

"Hey, girl," Tarah said. "Well, don't you look down in the mouth. What's got you lookin' that way?"

It was hard for Darcy to meet new people, especially someone like Tarah, a person Aunt Charlotte would call "low class." These were people who were loud and rude. They drank too much, used drugs, got into fights and ruined the neighborhood. They yelled ugly insults at people, even at their friends. Darcy did not actually know that Tarah did anything like this personally, but she seemed like the type who did.

"I just didn't think you'd be interested in tidal pools," Darcy explained.

Tarah slammed her big hand on the desk, making her gold bracelets jangle like ice cubes in a glass, and laughed. Darcy had never heard a mule bray, but she was sure it made exactly the same sound. Then Tarah leaned close and whispered, "Girl, I don't know a tidal pool from a fool. Ms. Reed stuck us together to mess with our heads, you hear what I'm sayin'?"

"Maybe we could switch to other partners," Darcy said nervously.

A big smile spread slowly over Tarah's face. "Nah, I think I'm gonna enjoy this. You're always sittin' here like a princess collecting your A's. Now you gotta work with a regular person, so you better loosen up, girl!"

Darcy felt as if her teeth were glued to her tongue. She fumbled in her bag for her outline of the project. It all seemed like a horrible joke now. She and Tarah Carson standing knee-deep in the muck of a tidal pool!

"Worms live there, don't they?" Tarah asked, twisting a big gold ring on her chubby finger.

"Yeah, I guess," Darcy replied.

"Big green worms," Tarah continued. "So if you get your feet stuck in the bottom of that old tidal pool, and you can't get out, do the worms crawl up your clothes?"

Darcy ignored the remark. "I'd like for us to go there soon, you know, look around."

"My boyfriend, Cooper, he goes down to the ocean all the time. He can take us. He says he's seen these fiddler crabs. They look like big spiders, and they'll try to bite your toes off. Cooper says so," Tarah said.

"Stop being silly," Darcy shot back. "If you're not even going to be serious . . . "

"You think you're better than me, don't you?" Tarah suddenly growled.

"I never said—" Darcy blurted.

"You don't have to say it, girl. It's in your eyes. You think I'm a low-life and you're something special. Well, I got more friends than you got fingers and toes together. You got no friends, and everybody laughs at you behind your back. Know what the word on you is? Darcy Wills give you the chills."

Just then, the bell rang, and Darcy was glad for the excuse to turn away from Tarah, to hide the hot tears welling in her eyes. She quickly rushed from the classroom, relieved that school was over. Darcy did not think she could bear to sit through another class just now.

Darcy headed down the long street towards home. She did not like Tarah . Maybe it was wrong, but it was true. Still, Tarah's brutal words hurt. Even stupid, awful people might tell you the truth about yourself. And Darcy did not have any real friends, except for Brisana. Maybe the other kids were mocking her behind her back. Darcy was very slender, not as shapely as many of the other girls. She remembered the time when Cooper Hodden was hanging in front of the deli with his friends, and he yelled as Darcy went by, "Hey, is that really a female there? Sure don't look like it. Looks more like an old broomstick with hair. " His companions laughed rudely, and Darcy had walked a little faster.

A terrible thought clawed at Darcy. Maybe she was the loser, not Tarah. Tarah was always hanging with a bunch of kids, laughing and joking. She would go down the hall to the lockers and greetings would come from everywhere. "Hey, Tarah!" "What's up, Tar?" "See ya at lunch, girl." When Darcy went to the lockers, there was dead silence.

Darcy usually glanced into stores on her way home from school. She enjoyed looking at the trays of chicken feet and pork ears at the little Asian grocery store. Sometimes she would even steal a glance at the diners sitting by the picture window at the Golden Grill Restaurant. But today she stare d straight ahead, her shoulders drooping.

If this had happened last year, she would have gone directly to Grandma's house, a block from where Darcy lived. How many times had Darcy and Jamee run to Grandma's, eaten applesauce cookies, drunk cider, and poured out their troubles to Grandma. Somehow, their problems would always dissolve in the warmth of her love and wisdom. But now Grandma was a frail figure in the corner of their apartment, saying little. And what little she did say made less and less sense.

Darcy was usually the first one home. The minute she got there, Mom left for the hospital to take the 3:00 to 11:00 shift in the ER. By the time Mom finished her paperwork at the hospital, she would be lucky to be home again by midnight. After Mom left, Darcy went to Grandma's room to give her the malted nutrition drink that the doctor ordered her to have three times a day.

"Want to drink your chocolate malt, Grandma?" Darcy asked, pulling up a chair beside Grandma's bed.

Grandma was sitting up, and her eyes were open. "No. I'm not hungry," she said listlessly. She always said that.

"You need to drink your malt, Grandma," Darcy insisted, gently putting the straw between the pinched lips.

Grandma sucked the malt slowly. "Grandma, nobody likes me at school," Darcy said. She did not expect any response. But there was a strange comfort in telling Grandma anyway. "Everybody laughs at me. It's because I'm shy and maybe stuck-up, too, I guess. But I don't mean to be. Stuck-up, I mean. Maybe I'm weird. I could be weird, I guess. I could be like Aunt Charlotte . . ." Tears rolled down Darcy's cheeks. Her heart ached with loneliness. There was nobody to talk to anymore, nobody who had time to listen, nobody who understood.

Grandma blinked and pushed the straw away. Her eyes brightened as they did now and then. "You are a wonderful girl. Everybody knows that," Grandma said in an almost normal voice. It happened like that sometimes. It was like being in the middle of a dark storm and having the clouds part, revealing a patch of clear, sunlit blue. For just a few precious minutes, Grandma was bright-eyed and saying normal things.

"Oh, Grandma, I'm so lonely," Darcy cried, pressing her head against Grandma's small shoulder.

"You were such a beautiful baby," Grandma said, stroking her hair." 'That one is going to shine like the morning star.' That's what I told your Mama. 'That child is going to shine like the morning star.' Tell me, Angelcake, is your daddy home yet?"

Darcy straightened. "Not yet." Her heart pounded so hard, she could feel it thumping in her chest. Darcy's father had not been home in five years.

"Well, tell him to see me when he gets home. I want him to buy you that blue dress you liked in the store window. That's for you, Angelcake. Tell him I've got money. My social security came, you know. I have money for the blue dress," Grandma said, her eyes slipping shut.

Just then, Darcy heard the apartment door slam. Jamee had come home. Now she stood in the hall, her hands belligerently on her hips. "Are you talking to Grandma again?" Jamee demanded.

"She was talking like normal," Darcy said. "Sometimes she does. You know she does."

"That is so stupid," Jamee snapped. "She never says anything right anymore. Not anything!" Jamee's voice trembled.

Darcy got up quickly and set down the can of malted milk. She ran to Jamee and put her arms around her sister. "Jamee, I know you're hurting too."

"Oh, don't be stupid," Jamee protested, but Darcy hugged her more tightly, and in a few seconds Jamee was crying. "She was the best thing in this stupid house," Jamee cried. "Why'd she have to go?"

"She didn't go," Darcy said. "Not really."

"She did! She did!" Jamee sobbed. She struggled free of Darcy, ran to her room, and slammed the door. In a minute, Darcy heard the bone-rattling sound of rap music.

Lost and Found, a Bluford Series™ novel, is reprinted with permission from Townsend Press. Copyright © 2002.

Want to read more? This and other *Bluford Series*™ novels and paperbacks can be purchased for $1 each at www.townsendpress.com.

Teens:
How to Get More Out of This Book

Self-help: The teens who wrote the stories in this book did so because they hope that telling their stories will help readers who are facing similar challenges. They want you to know that you are not alone, and that taking specific steps can help you manage or overcome very difficult situations. They've done their best to be clear about the actions that worked for them so you can see if they'll work for you.

Writing: You can also use the book to improve your writing skills. Each teen in this book wrote 5-10 drafts of his or her story before it was published. If you read the stories closely you'll see that the teens work to include a beginning, a middle, and an end, and good scenes, description, dialogue, and anecdotes (little stories). To improve your writing, take a look at how these writers construct their stories. Try some of their techniques in your own writing.

Reading: Finally, you'll notice that we include the first chapter from a Bluford Series novel in this book, alongside the true stories by teens. We hope you'll like it enough to continue reading. The more you read, the more you'll strengthen your reading skills. Teens at Youth Communication like the Bluford novels because they explore themes similar to those in their own stories. Your school may already have the Bluford books. If not, you can order them online for only $1.

Resources on the Web

We will occasionally post Think About It questions on our website, www.youthcomm.org, to accompany stories in this and other Youth Communication books. We try out the questions with teens and post the ones they like best. Many teens report that writing answers to those questions in a journal is very helpful.

How to Use This Book in Staff Training

Staff say that reading these stories gives them greater insight into what teens are thinking and feeling, and new strategies for working with them. You can help the staff you work with by using these stories as case studies.

Select one story to read in the group, and ask staff to identify and discuss the main issue facing the teen. There may be disagreement about this, based on the background and experience of staff. That is fine. One point of the exercise is that teens have complex lives and needs. Adults can probably be more effective if they don't focus too narrowly and can see several dimensions of their clients.

Ask staff: What issues or feelings does the story provoke in them? What kind of help do they think the teen wants? What interventions are likely to be most promising? Least effective? Why? How would you build trust with the teen writer? How have other adults failed the teen, and how might that affect his or her willingness to accept help? What other resources would be helpful to this teen, such as peer support, a mentor, counseling, family therapy, etc.

Resources on the Web

From time to time we will post Think About It questions on our website, www.youthcomm.org, to accompany stories in this and other Youth Communication books. We try out the questions with teens and post the ones that they find most effective. We'll also post lesson for some of the stories. Adults can use the questions and lessons in workshops.

Discussion Guide

Teachers and Staff:
How to Use This Book in Groups

When working with teens individually or in groups, using these stories can help young people face difficult issues in a way that feels safe to them. That's because talking about the issues in the stories usually feels safer to teens than talking about those same issues in their own lives. Addressing issues through the stories allows for some personal distance; they hit close to home, but not too close. Talking about them opens up a safe place for reflection. As teens gain confidence talking about the issues in the stories, they usually become more comfortable talking about those issues in their own lives.

Below are general questions that can help you lead discussions about the stories, which help teens and staff reflect on the issues in their own work and lives. In most cases you can read a story and conduct a discussion in one 45-minute session. Teens are usually happy to read the stories aloud, with each teen reading a paragraph or two. (Allow teens to pass if they don't want to read.) It takes 10-15 minutes to read a story straight through. However, it is often more effective to let workshop participants make comments and discuss the story as you go along. The workshop leader may even want to annotate her copy of the story beforehand with key questions.

If teens read the story ahead of time or silently, it's good to break the ice with a few questions that get everyone on the same page: Who is the main character? How old is she? What happened to her? How did she respond? Etc. Another good starting question is: "What stood out for you in the story?" Go around the room and let each person briefly mention one thing.

Then move on to open-ended questions, which encourage participants to think more deeply about what the writers were feeling, the choices they faced, and they actions they took. There are no right or wrong answers to the open-ended questions. Open-ended questions encourage participants to think about how the themes, emotions and choices in the stories relate to their own lives. Here are some examples of open-ended questions that we have found to be effective. You can use variations of these questions with almost any story in this book.

—What main problem or challenge did the writer face?

—What choices did the teen have in trying to deal with the problem?

—Which way of dealing with the problem was most effective for the teen? Why?

—What strengths, skills, or resources did the teen use to address the challenge?

—If you were in the writer's shoes, what would you have done?

—What could adults have done better to help this young person?

—What have you learned by reading this story that you didn't know before?

—What, if anything, will you do differently after reading this story?

—What surprised you in this story?

—Do you have a different view of this issue, or see a different way of dealing with it, after reading this story? Why or why not?

Credits

The stories in this book originally appeared in the following Youth Communication publications:

"And Then She Was Gone," by Lishone Bowsky, *Represent*, March/April 2000

"Building Trust,Brick by Brick," by Manny S, *Represent*, March/April 2008

"When I had the Chance, I Turned it Down" by Natalie Kozakiewicz, *New Youth Connections*, March 2003

"Finding My Father," by Dominick Freeman, *Represent*, November/December 2005

"My Adoption Story: She Was White, I Was Black," by LeFonche Rawls, *Represent*, May/June 1996

"Clean Slate," by Natasha Santos, *Represent*, May/June 2004

"How Counseling Can Help You Adjust," by Tamara S, *Represent*, March/April 2008

"I Lost My Brother To Adoption," By Wunika Hicks, *Represent*, July/August 1993

"Why Do Siblings Get Separated Through Adoption?" by Wunika Hicks, *Represent*, July/August 1993

"How to Stay Connected," *Represent*, September/October 2002

"Saying No to Adoption," *Represent*, March/April 2008

"Two Moms in My Heart," by Eric Green, *Represent*, May/June 2004

"Losing My Everything," by Jarel Melendez, *Represent*, September/October 2006

"Adopt-a-Teen?" by Natalie Kozakiewicz, *Represent*, July/August 2002

"Looking for a Mother Who Won't Leave," by Anonymous, *Represent*, May/June 2004

"Adoptive Families Need Support," by Lishone Bowsky, *Represent*, March/April 2000

"More Than Love," *Represent*, March/April 2008

"Embracing My Daughter's Children," by Benvanje Kelley, *Represent*, September/October 2004

"A Family to Raise Her," by Jennifer Olensky, *Represent*, May/June 2001

About Youth Communication

Youth Communication, founded in 1980, is a nonprofit youth development program located in New York City whose mission is to teach writing, journalism, and leadership skills. The teenagers we train become writers for our websites and books and for two print magazines, *New Youth Connections*, a general-interest youth magazine, and *Represent*, a magazine by and for young people in foster care.

Each year, up to 100 young people participate in Youth Communication's school-year and summer journalism workshops where they work under the direction of full-time professional editors. Most are African American, Latino, or Asian, and many are recent immigrants. The opportunity to reach their peers with accurate portrayals of their lives and important self-help information motivates the young writers to create powerful stories.

Our goal is to run a strong youth development program in which teens produce high quality stories that inform and inspire their peers. Doing so requires us to be sensitive to the complicated lives and emotions of the teen participants while also providing an intellectually rigorous experience. We achieve that goal in the writing/teaching/editing relationship, which is the core of our program.

Our teaching and editorial process begins with discussions

between adult editors and the teen staff. In those meetings, the teens and the editors work together to identify the most important issues in the teens' lives and to figure out how those issues can be turned into stories that will resonate with teen readers.

Once story topics are chosen, students begin the process of crafting their stories. For a personal story, that means revisiting events in one's past to understand their significance for the future. For a commentary, it means developing a logical and persuasive point of view. For a reported story, it means gathering information through research and interviews. Students look inward and outward as they try to make sense of their experiences and the world around them and find the points of intersection between personal and social concerns. That process can take a few weeks or a few months. Stories frequently go through ten or more drafts as students work under the guidance of their editors, the way any professional writer does.

Many of the students who walk through our doors have uneven skills, as a result of poor education, living under extremely stressful conditions, or coming from homes where English is a second language. Yet, to complete their stories, students must successfully perform a wide range of activities, including writing and rewriting, reading, discussion, reflection, research, interviewing, and typing. They must work as members of a team and they must accept individual responsibility. They learn to provide constructive criticism, and to accept it. They engage in explorations of truthfulness, fairness, and accuracy. They meet deadlines. They must develop the audacity to believe that they have something important to say and the humility to recognize that saying it well is not a process of instant gratification. Rather, it usually requires a long, hard struggle through many discussions and much rewriting.

It would be impossible to teach these skills and dispositions as separate, disconnected topics, like grammar, ethics, or assertiveness. However, we find that students make rapid progress when they are learning skills in the context of an inquiry that is personally significant to them and that will benefit their peers.

When teens publish their stories—in *New Youth Connections* and *Represent*, on the web, and in other publications—they reach tens of thousands of teen and adult readers. Teachers, counselors, social workers, and other adults circulate the stories to young people in their classes and out-of-school youth programs. Adults tell us that teens in their programs—including many who are ordinarily resistant to reading—clamor for the stories. Teen readers report that the stories give them information they can't get anywhere else, and inspire them to reflect on their lives and open lines of communication with adults.

Writers usually participate in our program for one semester, though some stay much longer. Years later, many of them report that working here was a turning point in their lives—that it helped them acquire the confidence and skills that they needed for success in college and careers. Scores of our graduates have overcome tremendous obstacles to become journalists, writers, and novelists. They include National Book Award finalist Edwidge Danticat, novelist Ernesto Quinonez, writer Veronica Chambers and *New York Times* reporter Rachel Swarns. Hundreds more are working in law, business, and other careers. Many are teachers, principals, and youth workers, and several have started nonprofit youth programs themselves and work as mentors—helping another generation of young people develop their skills and find their voices.

Youth Communication is a nonprofit educational corporation. Contributions are gratefully accepted and are tax deductible to the fullest extent of the law.

To make a contribution, or for information about our publications and programs, including our catalog of over 100 books and curricula for hard-to-reach teens, see www.youthcomm.org

About The Editors

Al Desetta has been an editor of Youth Communication's two teen magazines, *Foster Care Youth United* (now known as *Represent*) and *New Youth Connections*. He was also an instructor in Youth Communication's juvenile prison writing program. In 1991, he became the organization's first director of teacher development, working with high school teachers to help them produce better writers and student publications.

Prior to working at Youth Communication, Desetta directed environmental education projects in New York City public high schools and worked as a reporter.

He has a master's degree in English literature from City College of the City University of New York and a bachelor's degree from the State University of New York at Binghamton, and he was a Revson Fellow at Columbia University for the 1990-91 academic year.

He is the editor of many books, including several other Youth Communication anthologies: *The Heart Knows Something Different: Teenage Voices from the Foster Care System*, *The Struggle to Be Strong*, and *The Courage to Be Yourself*. He is currently a freelance editor.

Keith Hefner co-founded Youth Communication in 1980 and has directed it ever since. He is the recipient of the Luther P. Jackson Education Award from the New York Association of Black Journalists and a MacArthur Fellowship. He was also a Revson Fellow at Columbia University.

Laura Longhine is the editorial director at Youth Communication. She edited *Represent*, Youth Communication's magazine by and for youth in foster care, for three years, and has written for a variety of publications. She has a BA in English from Tufts University and an MS in Journalism from Columbia University.

More Helpful Books From Youth Comunication

Do You Have What It Takes? A Comprehensive Guide to Success After Foster Care. In this survival manual, current and former foster teens show how they prepared not only for the practical challenges they've faced on the road to independence, but also the emotional ones. Worksheets and exercises help foster teens plan for their future. Activity pages at the end of each chapter help social workers, independent living instructors, and other leaders use the stories with individuals or in groups. (Youth Communication)

The Struggle to Be Strong: True Stories by Teens About Overcoming Tough Times. Foreword by Veronica Chambers. Help young people identify and build on their own strengths with 30 personal stories about resiliency. (Free Spirit)

Depression, Anger, Sadness: Teens Write About Facing Difficult Emotions. Give teens the confidence they need to seek help when they need it. These teens write candidly about difficult emotional problems—such as depression, cutting, and domestic violence—and how they have tried to help themselves. (Youth Communication)

What Staff Need to Know: Teens Write About What Works. How can foster parents, group home staff, caseworkers, social workers, and teachers best help teens? These stories show how communication can be improved on both sides, and provide insight into what kinds of approaches and styles work best. (Youth Communication)

Out of the Shadows: Teens Write About Surviving Sexual Abuse. Help teens feel less alone and more hopeful about overcoming the trauma of sexual abuse. This collection includes first-person accounts by male and female survivors grappling with fear, shame, and guilt. (Youth Communication)

Just the Two of Us: Teens Write About Building Good Relationships. Show teens how to make and maintain healthy relationships (and avoid bad ones). Many teens in care have had poor role models and are emotionally vulnerable. These stories demonstrate good and bad choices teens make in friendship and romance. (Youth Communication)

The Fury Inside: Teens Write About Anger. Help teens manage their anger. These writers show how they got better control of their emotions and sought the support of others. (Youth Communication)

Always on the Move: Teens Write About Changing Homes and Staff. Help teens feel less alone with these stories about how their peers have coped with the painful experience of frequent placement changes, and turnover among staff and social workers. (Youth Communication)

My Secret Addiction: Teens Write About Cutting. These true accounts of cutting, or self-mutilation, offer a window into the personal and family situations that lead to this secret habit, and show how teens can get the help they need. (Youth Communication)

Growing Up Together: Teens Write About Being Parents. Give teens a realistic view of the conflicts and burdens of parenthood with these stories from real teen parents. The stories also reveal how teens grew as individuals by struggling to become responsible parents. (Youth Communication)

To order these and other books, go to:
www.youthcomm.org
or call 212-279-0708 x115

www.ingramcontent.com/pod-product-compliance
Lightning Source LLC
Chambersburg PA
CBHW071729090426
42738CB00011B/2425